Paul Celan was one of the most important poets to write in German and, in the words of George Steiner, 'almost certainly the major European poet of the period after 1945'. He was born in 1920 into a Jewish family in Bukovina, a German enclave in Romania that was destroyed by the Nazis. Although both his parents were killed in the Holocaust, Celan managed to escape, and he spent most of his productive years in France. In Paris he wrote his poetry and translated the work of Rimbaud, Shakespeare, Emily Dickinson, Blok and Mandelstam, among others. The first book of his own poems was published in Germany in 1952, and he soon began to receive widespread recognition.

Language, Paul Celan said, was the only thing that remained intact for him after the war. His experiences of the war years and of the loss of his parents are the recurrent themes of his poetry. He died, a suicide by drowning, in 1970 at the age of forty-nine.

Michael Hamburger has written, translated and edited across the fields of German, French, Italian and Romanian literature. Educated at Westminster and Christ Church, Oxford, he lectured at University College, London and the University of Reading, and has held visiting posts at universities and colleges in America and Great Britain. He has received many awards and honours including two honorary doctorates, several prizes for his translations and, in 1992, an OBE. He has produced poetry throughout his writing life, his *Collected Poems 1941–1994* being published in 1995 and his critical work on the subject, *The Truth of Poetry*, in 1970, by Penguin. He has also written his memoirs, *String of Beginnings* (1991), and published many critical works and translations.

CELAN: SELECTED POEMS

Paul Celan was one of the most important poets to write in German and, in the words of George Steiner, 'almost certainly the major European poet of the period after 1945'. He was born in 1920 into a Jewish family in Bukovina, a German enclave in Romania that was destroyed by the Nazis. Although both his parents were killed in the Holocaust, Celan managed to escape, and he spent most of his productive years in France. In Paris he wrote his poetry and translated the work of Rimbaud, Shakespeare, Emily Dickinson, Blok and Mandelstam, among others. The first book of his own poems was published in Germany in 1952, and he soon began to receive widespread recognition.

Language, Paul Celan said, was the only thing that remained intact for him after the war. His experience of the war years and of the loss of his parents are the recurrent themes of his poetry. He died, a suicide by drowning, in 1970 at the age of forty-nine.

Michael Hamburger has written, translated and edited across the fields of German, French, Italian and Romanian literature. Educated at Westminster and Christ Church, Oxford, he lectured at University College, London and the University of Reading, and has held visiting posts at universities and colleges in America and Great Britain. He has received many awards and honours including two honorary doctorates, several prizes for his translations and, in 1992, an OBE. He has produced poetry throughout his writing life, his Collected Poems 1941–1994 being published in 1995 and his critical work on the subject, The Truth of Poetry, in 1970 by Penguin. He has also written his memoirs, String of Beginnings (1991), and published many critical works and translations.

PAUL CELAN

SELECTED POEMS

TRANSLATED
WITH AN INTRODUCTION BY
MICHAEL HAMBURGER

PENGUIN BOOKS

PENGUIN BOOKS

Published by the Penguin Group
Penguin Books Ltd, 27 Wrights Lane, London W8 5TZ, England
Penguin Putnam Inc., 375 Hudson Street, New York, New York 10014, USA
Penguin Books Australia Ltd, Ringwood, Victoria, Australia
Penguin Books Canada Ltd, 10 Alcorn Avenue, Toronto, Ontario, Canada M4V 3B2
Penguin Books (NZ) Ltd, Private Bag 102902, NSMC, Auckland, New Zealand

Penguin Books Ltd, Registered Offices: Harmondsworth, Middlesex, England

First published by Anvil Press Poetry 1988
Published in Penguin Books 1990
Revised edition published by Anvil Press Poetry 1995
Published in Penguin Books 1996

018

Introduction and translations copyright © Michael Hamburger, 1972, 1980, 1988, 1995

Grateful acknowledgement is made to the publishers of the following editions of
Paul Celan's poems for permission to reprint the German texts: *Mohn und
Gedächtnis* and *Von Schwelle zu Schwelle* copyright © Deutsche Verlags-Anstalt
GmbH, Stuttgart, 1952 & 1955; *Sprachgitter* and *Die Niemandsrose* copyright
© S. Fischer Verlag, Frankfurt am Main, 1959 & 1963; *Atemwende, Fadensonnen,
Lichtzwang, Schneepart* and *Zeitgehöft* copyright © Suhrkamp Verlag, Frankfurt
am Main, 1967, 1968, 1970, 1971, 1976.

Acknowledgements are also due to the following publications, in which
some of the translations first appeared: *Chicago Review, Decade* (Boston),
European Judaism (London), *Exile* (Toronto), *PN Review, Poetry* (Chicago),
Poetry Review, Stand, 2 Plus 2 (Switzerland) and *Paul Celan 32 Poems*
(Embers Handpress, Norwich, 1985).

Filmset in Ehrhardt Monotype
Printed in England by Clays Ltd, St Ives plc

ISBN 978-0-14-018920-9

www.greenpenguin.co.uk

Poems of Paul Celan

Inhalt

Contents

from ATEMWENDE (1967)

from ATEMWENDE (1967)

Wirk nicht voraus

from SCHNEEPART (1971)

from ZEITGEHÖFT (1976)

Preface

To THIS NEW EDITION I have been able to add only two new translations. A third would have been added – if only in the Introduction – if it had not been of a poem withheld by Celan from his collections and not available yet for publication either in the original or in translation.

Crucial corrections have been made in four versions previously included. In my lecture "On Translating Celan" (*Testimonies*, 1989) I gave an account of the extreme difficulties of rendering one short poem, "Coagula". It was only after that lecture and the publication of my version of the poem that I realized I had got it wrong, after all the deliberation, researches and agonizing over a single word in it. Of all the five or more quite different meanings of the German word "Kolben", I had missed what I now believe to be the primary one in the context, failing to connect the political layer of the poem with the alchemical, intimated in the title.

A different kind of error – one of misreading – occurred in my version of "Todtnauberg". My resort to the almost archaic word "fascine" – owed to a dictionary, like many words in Celan's own poems – was explained and justified in a contribution to *The Independent* (22 December 1990), where the corrected version first appeared. It is to my friend Franz Wurm that I owe the correction in "For a Brother in Asia". In a letter he pointed out to me that in the last line Celan played on a wholly archaic, formerly idiomatic, sense of the verb "ersterben".

My Introduction to this book should make clear why I call these corrections "crucial". Every word in Celan's later poems is crucial. If a crucial word also has several possible meanings, and not all these meanings can be conveyed in a translation, it was up to me to find the primary one in the context. That is why the correcting of my versions was as slow and gradual a process as the translating itself has been.

M. H.
August, 1994

Introduction

development in German poetry that runs
Hölderlin in the eighteenth century to the present time and being
Trakl, at a time when the dominant trends in both Germanys
were adverse to that line. Bobrowski is on record as disliking and

FROM WHATEVER direction we approach it – as plain readers of
poetry, as critics or literary historians, as biographers or
sociologists, or as translators – Paul Celan's work confronts us
with difficulty and paradox. The more we try to concentrate on
the poem itself, on its mode of utterance, which includes both
theme and manner, the more we are made aware that difficulty
and paradox are of its essence. As for "placing" his work within
the body of German imaginative literature after 1945, or against
the larger background of international modernism, all we can be
certain of at this point is that it occupies a prominent, isolated,
and anomalous position. With Nelly Sachs this German poet,
born of a Jewish family in Romania, shared an obvious pre-
occupation with the mass killings he had physically survived but
could never recover from; and a not so obvious immersion in
Jewish history and religious – especially mystical – tradition. Yet,
apart from their differences in poetic practice, Nelly Sachs had
been a German poet before persecution turned her into a Jewish
one. Like other assimilated German Jews, she had to look for
her Jewish roots – with the help of Gentile friends, as it hap-
pened. Celan, too, had written juvenile poems in German before
he was marked for life by the events of the war years – a facsimile
edition of Celan's holograph collection of such poems written
between 1938 and 1944 was published in 1985 – but the incep-
tion of his characteristic work dates from the news of his
mother's violent death, reported to him in the winter of 1943.

Paul Celan spent his formative years in a Jewish community
that had recently ceased to be within the frontiers of the Aus-
trian Empire; and most of his productive years were spent in
France. His poetic affinities were French, Romanian, Russian
and English, as well as German and Austrian. Among his
German-language contemporaries, those closest to him in
sensibility and manner – though that is not saying much –
were Johannes Bobrowski, a resident in East Berlin with dis-
tinctly Christian allegiances, and the West German poet Ernst
Meister. Like them, Celan can be seen as continuing a line of

development in German poetry that runs from Klopstock and Hölderlin in the eighteenth century to the later Rilke and Georg Trakl, at a time when the dominant trends in both Germanys were adverse to that line. Bobrowski is on record as disliking and rejecting Celan's later work; but he included two poems of Celan's middle years in the anthology of his favourite German poems he compiled for his own use, with no obligation or reason, therefore, to make it representative. (This anthology was published posthumously in 1985 as *Meine liebsten Gedichte*.) The affinity, as far as it goes, could be real even if neither Bobrowski nor Meister had acknowledged it. Yet it offers no significant point of entry into Celan's work. Literary scholars are still in the process of tracing Celan's imagery to the books he read, the life he led, the places he visited, of unravelling his complex concerns and uncovering the sources of many seemingly cryptic allusions in his poems.

As a translator I have profited by these scholarly researches, which have become so numerous, extensive and heterogeneous that I cannot acknowledge my debts specifically, though I should like to thank one Celan scholar, Dietlind Meinecke, for reading my earlier versions and questioning some of my interpretations. I am also grateful to Alfred Kittner, a poet born in Celan's home town, for providing me with biographical clues to one perplexing poem. Much of Celan's later poetry can be intuitively grasped, but not rendered in another language, without as much knowledge as possible of his sources; and any help a translator can get from scholars makes it that much more penetrable. Yet it is as a translator, too, that I insist on the essential difficulty and paradox of his poetry. These can be illumined, but not resolved or dissolved, by scholarly research. It is the difficulty and the paradox that demand a special attention to every word in his texts, and this attention is something other than what is normally meant by "understanding". I am by no means sure that I have "understood" even those of his poems – a small proportion of his output – which I have been able to translate over the years; but every time I return to his poems, with or without the help offered by their interpreters, this or that poem, left untranslated before, suddenly becomes translatable. This has to do with the precision and reliability of Celan's later work. Despite the "darkness" that belongs to it, necessarily and genetically, despite the characteristic leaps and bounds of his poems, their haltingness and their silences, nothing in them is slapdash or vague, nothing is meaningless, nothing has been left to chance or to merely emotive gestures. What makes them difficult is the terrain itself – a terrain in which milk is black, death is the all-encompassing reality – not the nature of its charting.

Paul Antschel – then Ancel, then Celan, an anagram adopted in 1947, when his first poems appeared in a Romanian periodical – was born at Czernowitz (now Chernovtsy) in Bukovina on 23 November 1920. After his schooling there, he paid his first visit to France in 1938 as a medical student at Tours, but returned to his home town in the following year to study Romance languages and literatures. In June 1940 Czernowitz was occupied by Soviet troops, but Celan was able to continue his studies until 1941, when German and Romanian forces occupied the region and the Jews were herded into a ghetto. At this period he learned Russian and began to translate poems by Yesenin. In the summer of 1942 his parents were deported to an internment camp in Transnistria, where his father died of typhus and his mother was murdered later by a shot in the neck. Paul Celan managed to escape arrest until conscripted for labour service in Southern Moldavia, where he worked on road building. On a short leave to Czernowitz he stayed with his grandfather, then with the parents of his friend Edith Horowitz. In February 1944 the Romanian labour camp was dissolved, and Celan returned to Bukovina, which had been re-occupied by the Soviets and annexed to the Ukraine. For a time he is reported to have worked as a "field surgeon" in a psychiatric unit. Then he took up his studies again until April 1945, when he left the Soviet Union for Bucharest, working as a publisher's reader and translator of Russian texts into Romanian. (It was then that he adopted the spelling "Ancel" for his surname.) In December 1947 he succeeded in leaving Romania illegally for Vienna, but stayed there only until July of the following year. After the publication in Austria of his first book of poems, *Der Sand aus den Urnen*, which he withdrew because of the many misprints it contained, he settled in Paris, where he took up the study of German literature. In 1950 he obtained his "Licence" and became a lecturer in German literature at the École Normale Supérieure. After his marriage in 1952 to the graphic artist Gisèle Lestrange – who contributed etchings to several limited editions of poems by Celan – Paris remained his home until his suicide by drowning in the Seine in April 1970, at the age of forty-nine. The death in infancy of their first son, François, is commemorated in a poem included here. Celan's second son, Eric, survived his father.

Most of the poems in the rejected first collection, *Der Sand aus den Urnen*, were reprinted in *Mohn und Gedächtnis*, which appeared in West Germany in 1952 and won him immediate recognition, confirmed by an invitation to read at the annual gathering of the "Gruppe 47" in the same year. Celan's next collection *Von Schwelle zu Schwelle* followed in 1955. Between 1957 and 1967, Celan received a number of prizes, including the prestigious Georg Büchner Prize (awarded by the German Academy for Language and Literature, Darmstadt) in 1960. A speech delivered by Celan on that occasion, "Der Meridian",[1] is one of the very few prose pieces he published and his nearest approach, in terms hardly less idiosyncratic than the practice on which it comments, to a manifesto of his aims as a poet.

With the publication of *Sprachgitter* (1959) and *Die Niemandsrose* (1963), Celan's work moved into a second phase. These two central collections marked the height of his undisputed acclaim in the German-speaking world. For reasons that have to do not only with his subsequent development but with the almost exclusively political and social interests that became predominant in West German literature in the later sixties and early seventies, fewer and fewer of his readers and critics were prepared to follow him into what they regarded as the increasingly private world of his later poetry. His next books, *Atemwende* and *Fadensonnen*, had a mixed reception; and so did his three posthumous collections, *Lichtzwang*, *Schneepart* and *Zeitgehöft*.

Throughout his working life Celan was also active as a translator. His many translations from the French included poetry by

[1] For an English version of this, and Celan's few other prose works, see his *Collected Prose*, translated by Rosmarie Waldrop, Carcanet Press, Manchester, 1986.

Rimbaud, Valéry, Apollinaire, Michaux, Char, André du Bouchet, and Jean Daive. From the English he translated sonnets by Shakespeare and poems by Emily Dickinson and Marianne Moore; from the Russian, selections of poems by Blok, Yesenin, and Mandelstam. During his stay in Bucharest he had produced translations into Romanian of Russian prose works.

These basic facts of Celan's life – no book-length biography of him has yet appeared,[2] and very few biographical documents have been released for publication – may indicate something of the anomaly and extremity of his position as a poet. What the facts do not reveal, and his productivity may seem to belie, is that the loss of his parents and his early experience of persecution left indelible scars. Throughout his later years, he suffered acute crises and breakdowns that affected both his personal and his professional life. One such crisis occurred soon after his emergence as a poet, when Claire Goll, the widow of the Franco-German poet Yvan Goll, with whom Celan had become personally acquainted in 1949, accused Celan of having plagiarized Goll's work. Since Celan's early poems linked up with both German Expressionism and French Surrealism, movements with which Goll had been associated, certain stylistic features were bound to be common to the two poets. If Celan had not been predisposed towards paranoia, the foolish and protracted public controversies that ensued could not have hurt him; as it was, Claire Goll's maniacal accusations, renewed even after Celan's death and right up to her own, obsessed and unbalanced him. I recall a meeting with Celan when he was similarly obsessed with the "treachery" of one of his publishers, who had decided to reissue the poems of a ballad-writer popular during

[2] A biographical account of Celan's early years and family background appeared in 1979. It is *Paul Celan* by Israel Chalfen, Insel Verlag, Frankfurt. Another account, by Celan's Czernowitz friend Edith Silbermann, was published in the volume *Argumentum E Silentio*, International Celan Symposium, edited by Amy Colin, Walter de Gruyter, Berlin and New York, 1987. A special issue of the periodical *Zeitschrift für Kulturaustausch*, Vol. 32 No. 3, Stuttgart, 1982, contains other reminiscences of Celan's early years by Romanian friends. It is Celan's later life that has not been recorded in comparable detail.

the Nazi régime. Towards the end of his life, the crises became more violent and more disruptive.

Paul Celan had no wish to be a confessional poet, except in so far as all poets are confessional, because they must be true to their own experience. Even in the early "Death Fugue", his most famous and most widely anthologized poem, the personal anguish was transposed into distancing imagery and a musical structure so incompatible with reportage that a kind of "terrible beauty" is wrested from the ugly theme. Realists and literalists among Celan's critics were to object to his "aestheticizing" of the death camps. Yet the power and pathos of the poem arises from the extreme tension between its grossly impure material and its pure form. The impossibility of writing poems after Auschwitz, let alone about Auschwitz, has become a critical commonplace. Celan knew that even he could not hope to do so directly, realistically, but only by an art of contrast and allusion that celebrates beauty and energy while commemorating their destruction. Though he turned against his "Death Fugue" in later years, refusing permission to have it reprinted in more anthologies, that was because he had refined his art in the meantime to a point where the early poem seemed too direct, too explicit. Meanwhile, he had also found a place for ugliness in his poems – but in poems that were judged to be private and "hermetic". Yet the anguish, the darkness, the shadow of death are present in all his work, early and late, including the most high-spirited and sensuous.

The aspiration towards a pure or "absolute" poetry was pervasive in France after Mallarmé, among poets of almost every school, and it was not necessarily thought to be incompatible with political or moral commitments. Like Paul Eluard and René Char, of the French poets to whom Celan felt close, Celan resisted the constraint to sacrifice the freedom of his art to an "engagement" outside or beyond it. Celan's religious, ethical, or political commitments could become explicit at times, as in his poem in memory of Eluard, but more often they had to remain implicit. At his most difficult, most elliptic and paradoxical, he insisted that he was not a hermetic poet but one out to communicate, describing his poems as "ways of a voice to a receptive you", a "desperate dialogue", and "a sort of homecoming".

Another way of putting it is that his poetry never ceased to be rooted in experience, extreme experience that could not be enacted in any manner less difficult than his. The hiatuses, the silences, the dislocations of normal usage belong to what he had to say and to the effort of saying it.

If Celan had set out to write hermetic poems, his work would be less difficult than it is, because it would not require us to make the kind of sense of it that we know it can yield. That is why his earlier verse, though purer, is less difficult than the later. Any reader familiar with the kind of poetry whose progression is one of imagery rather than argument will know how to read the earlier poems, whose diction, too, is closer to established conventions. From *Sprachgitter* onwards the images grow sparser, more idiosyncratic, and more laden with conflict, the syntax more broken, the message at once more urgent and more reticent. The available resources of language and prosody become inadequate. Celan begins to coin new words, especially compound words, and to divide other words into their component syllables, each of which acquires a new weight. The process of condensation and dislocation is carried farther in the subsequent collections. Both verse lines and whole poems tend to be shorter and shorter.

One exception, the longer poem, "The Straitening", both records and exemplifies the change. Its German title, "Engführung", is a technical term for a device employed in the composition of fugues. Its counterpart in English usage would have been the Italian word *stretto*, "an artifice by which the subject and answer are, as it were, bound closer together, by being made to overlap" (SOED). This title recalls the precedent of Celan's earlier "Death Fugue", and a comparison between the two poems shows just how daring, cryptic, and spare Celan's manner had become in the interjacent thirteen years. Although the form of the later poem is an even closer approximation to fugal composition with words – an impossibility, of course, because words cannot be counterpointed if they are to remain intelligible – I decided not to use the technical term for the title. (The French translation by Jean Daive, which was authorized by Celan, does use the technical term, *Strette*.) A German reader of the original text not versed in specialized musical terminology would take the title more literally as a "narrowing down" or "reduction"; and since this wider, more general and more revealing connotation would not be conveyed by the strictly musical term, I looked for an English word that would at least suggest it. Ambiguity, in any case, occurs throughout the poem; and since Celan took every word as literally as possible, often breaking it down etymologically in the manner of Heidegger, one of his reasons for choosing the German word must have been that it characterized not only the structure of his poem but its theme as well, the development that drove Celan himself into his narrowest bounds and his utmost intensity.

The later poems included in my selection are those not rendered totally untranslatable by polysemy – to use an ugly neologism more accurate than "ambiguity" – play on words, or a degree of uncertainty as to what the poem is about that would have made translation little more than guesswork. It was a question not of whether I could catch this allusion or that – many must have escaped me even in poems that I did translate – but whether I could respond to the gesture of the poem as a whole. If the gesture of the poem came home to me, the oddities of diction and usage, including the ambiguities, could usually be conveyed in English, with certain modifications due to the different characters of the two languages. German, for instance, lends itself to the formation of compound words in a way that English does not. German verbs, too, can be given new directions, new functions, by combining them freely with prepositions like "in", "through", "into", "around", "after" – a freedom by which the later Rilke had profited as greatly as Celan did after him. German also permits nouns to be preceded by complete clauses that qualify them, a peculiarity of the language that was especially congenial to Celan when the movement of his poem had come to be governed by breath units rather than metrical or syntactical units:

Und du:
du, du, du
mein täglich wahr- und wahrer-
geschundenes Später
der Rosen –:

where the German capitalization of nouns helps to bring out that the adverb "später" has been turned into a noun. This had to be transposed as follows:

> And you:
> you, you, you
> my later of roses
> daily worn true and
> more true —:

A structurally faithful rendering would have demanded:

> And you:
> you, you, you
> my daily true- and truer-
> worn later
> of (the) roses —:

with the additional substitution of a stronger word than "worn" to convey the sense of abuse and maltreatment contained in the German word "geschunden".

Those lines are from a poem of Celan's middle period. More puzzling innovations abound in the later collections, as in this short poem, "Once":

> ONCE
> I heard him,
> he was washing the world,
> unseen, nightlong,
> real.
>
> One and Infinite,
> annihilated,
> ied.
>
> Light was. Salvation.

The German word corresponding to "ied" is "ichten". Since it comes after "vernichtet" (annihilated) it could be the infinitive of a verb that is the positive counterpart of "annihilate", and that is how it was construed by a reviewer for *The Times Literary Supplement*, who translated it as "ihilate". This new verb would not be more far-fetched than other neologisms of Celan's, since in the Middle High German, which he knew, there was a positive "iht" (ought) corresponding to the negative "niht" (nought). My authority for "ied" is Paul Celan himself. When I last met him, in April 1968, he was convinced that I was the author of the anonymous *TLS* review and would not accept my repeated denial. He explained that "ichten" was formed from the personal pronoun "ich", so that it was the third person plural of the imperfect tense of a verb "ichen", (to i).

An equally ambiguous word formation occurs in the poem "Etched away", but Celan did not comment on the translation offered by the same reviewer of *Atemwende*. I refer to

> ... das hundert-
> züngige Mein-
> gedicht, das Genicht.

rendered there as

> ... the hundred-
> tongued my-
> poem, the noem.

"Mein-gedicht" could indeed mean "my-poem", but it could also mean "false poem" or "pseudo-poem", by analogy with the German word "Meineid", a false oath. Probably Celan had both senses in mind when he coined the word. In this case translation had to resolve the ambiguity, and after much pondering I decided in favour of "pseudo-poem", although "Meineid" is the only modern German word that retains this sense of "mein". Paul Celan was a learned poet with an outstandingly rich vocabulary derived more from reading than from practice in the vernacular – inevitably, considering how little time he spent in German-speaking countries. The retention of that root in a single modern word is the kind of thing that would have struck and intrigued him no less than the ambiguity of "my" and "false" in that syllable.

Celan's interest in Yiddish usage also brought him up against the medieval roots of the German language. Like other twentieth-century poets, such as W. H. Auden or Francis Ponge, he must have been fascinated by dictionaries, especially etymological ones. What is certain is that he both loved and mistrusted words to a degree that has to do with his anomalous position as a poet born in a German-speaking enclave that had been destroyed by the Germans. His German could not and must not be the German of the destroyers. That is one reason why he had to make a new language for himself, a language at once probing and groping, critical and innovative; and why the richer his verbal and formal resources grew, the more strictly he confined them to the orbit of his most urgent concerns.

These permitted no separation of Celan's personal experience from the larger implications it held for him, no convenient division into a private and public *persona*. That is why a full documentation of Celan's life is needed for the elucidation of many of his later poems – and why he was perfectly right to insist that he was not a hermetic poet. ("Ganz und gar nicht hermetisch" – "absolutely not hermetic" – are his words in the copy of *Die Niemandsrose* he inscribed for me.) An interpretation of a late poem of Celan's by the distinguished critic Peter Szondi – who was close to Celan and followed him into suicide soon after writing the essay in question, "Eden", in 1971 – unlocks the imagery of that poem only by virtue of knowing what Celan saw, read, and talked about on his visit to Berlin in December 1967. The poem "Du liegst" from *Schneepart* combines allusions to the murder of Karl Liebknecht and Rosa Luxemburg, and the throwing of Rosa Luxemburg's corpse into the Landwehrkanal – a political theme, that is – with details of Christmas street scenes that had struck Celan during his visit. Szondi's elucidation of the double or triple meanings of the operative words in that poem might have enabled me to translate it, but not to make those meanings accessible to English-language readers without notes; and one link in the triple rhyme of the poem – "Schweden-Eden-jeden" – could not be reproduced in English. So I chose not to translate the poem.

Another late poem, included here, makes a more public and explicit connection between historical events separated by nearly two millennia. It is "Think of It", from *Fadensonnen*. The poem not only associates, but fuses, the last attempt of the Jews to hold out against the Romans at Massada in 70 A.D., which ended with the suicide of those besieged in the fortress there, with the Prussian concentration camp at Börgermoor, whose inmates composed the song known as the "Börgermoor-Lied". This song gave them a sense of group identity, in the teeth of group extermination, and was finally adopted even by the German guards at the camp. Celan's poem, then, celebrates the only kind of victory – a moral one – available to the defenders of Massada and the inmates of Börgermoor; and it was characteristic of him to do so not by comparing and explaining the two events but by presenting them as a dual event, in his own, most intimately personal, terms. Celan chose not to help his readers by providing clues to any of his poems in the form of notes. Very few of his German readers, for instance, could possibly be expected to know that Mapesbury Road – the title of another late poem – is a street in north-west London where Celan used to visit a surviving relative, his father's sister, who is addressed in the poem.

To understand the poem "Todtnauberg" (from *Lichtzwang*) we have to know that its title is the name of the place where Martin Heidegger lived; and that Celan found it possible to maintain an intense intellectual relationship with Heidegger despite the philosopher's notorious record of public support for the Hitler régime, and Heidegger's adamant refusal, right up to his death, to take back one word he had spoken or written in praise of the régime. Celan's poem enacts his hope that Heidegger might, after all, speak the word that would acknowledge the survivor's wound – an act of atonement, if not of healing, since Celan's wound could not be healed. As ever, the enactment is an indirect, symbolic one, conveyed in images of the well, the wild flowers, and the book. The plant whose English name is "eyebright" or "euphrasy" is called "Augentrost" (literally "eyecomfort") in German; and the significance of eyes and seeing in Celan's poetry needs no comment. The flower's name alone gives the botanical reality – and Celan had been a keen practical botanist since his early youth – its full poetic charge. (In medieval times the plant was used to cure diseases of the eye.) The book of the poem is Heidegger's visitors' book, with entries going back to the period in question between the two men. Celan's entry in the book is an intimation of his hope, but for which he could not have inscribed the book at all. As ever, too, each tiniest detail in the poem is meaningful, though the meaning is one that lies in the complex and subtle interactions between literal data and their symbolic extension.

Literalists could object that in one of Celan's last poems, "Die Posaunenstelle", I have mistranslated "Posaune" ("trombone") as "trumpet". Again it is a matter not of literal rendering but of interpretation. An interpretation of this poem by Bernhard Böschenstein has shown that it alludes to the "seven angels which had the seven trumpets" in Revelations 8. In the Lutheran German Bible those trumpets are trombones, but the allusion – cryptic enough, as it is – would be totally obscured by a literal rendering in English. For the same reason Celan's "Fackel" ("torch") in that poem is rendered as "lamp": "And the third angel sounded, and there fell a great star from heaven, burning as it were a lamp, and it fell upon the third part of the rivers, and upon the fountains of waters" – where Luther's version has a torch instead of a lamp. These allusions are crucial. Amongst other things they mark the apocalyptic extremities that Celan's negative theology had reached, and the extent to which his preoccupations bore on Christian, as well as Jewish, tradition. Even here the negation – the "lacuna" or "time hole" – is not absolute. There is a suggestion that the emptiness can and must be filled.

Negation is a strikingly recurrent feature not only of Celan's new word formations but of his later poetry in general. The seemingly negative theology of his great poem "Psalm" has been shown to have antecedents in both Jewish and Christian mysticism, and Celan is known to have been well versed in both. Less explicitly than in "Psalm", something of this theology is prefigured even in very early poems, as is the related dialectic of light and darkness that runs through all of Celan's work. Celan's religion – and there can be no doubt as to his profoundly religious sensibility, whatever he may have believed or not believed – had to come to grips with the experience of being God-forsaken. Negation and blasphemy were the means by which Celan could be true to that experience and yet maintain the kind of intimate dialogue with God characteristic of Jewish devotion.

At the same time negation and paradox served him as a basic stylistic principle, as expounded in the early poem "Speak, You Also". In that poem he exhorts himself to "keep yes and no unsplit", to admit enough darkness into his poems, because "he speaks truly who speaks the shade." With its dialectic of light and dark, life and death, this poem anticipates the whole of Celan's subsequent development, as well as linking the formal aspects of that development – the reduction carried farther from book to book – with the inner necessity from which they arose: "Thinner you grow, less knowable, finer." This applies to the poems as much as to the poet; and so does the star image, towards the end of the poem, that stands for the urge towards transcendence and resolution of paradox present in Celan's work right up to the posthumous collections.

One thing sets Paul Celan's work apart from that of most of his German coevals: he had hardly any use for realism of a kind that merely imitates and reproduces, for what Northrop Frye has called "the low mimetic". Direct social comment is not to be found in his work, though it became increasingly realistic in a different sense – the widening of its vocabulary to include twentieth-century phenomena and technologies. From *Die Niemandsrose* onwards, invective becomes prominent in Celan's poems, though the invective is as rich in cryptic allusions and intricate word-play as every other mode that he employed. He was realistic, too, in doing full justice to "the foul rag-and-bone shop of the heart". Yet he was never satisfied with mere reportage. As a very short late poem attests, he found Brecht's poetry of social and political comment too "explicit". One reason is that he wanted poetry to be open to the unexpected, the unpredictable, the unpredeterminable. His poems were "messages in a bottle", as he said, which might or might not be picked up. That element of risk was as necessary to them as the need to communicate. On the few occasions when he spoke about poetry in public he spoke of it as a process, a groping forward, a search. Paradoxically, once more, he spoke of its practice, and the practice of any art, as a driving of the practitioner into the "inmost recess of himself", his narrowest place, and as a "setting free". It is this peculiarity I had in mind when choosing not to translate his title "Engführung" as "Stretto".

No feature of Celan's later poems is more characteristic of their openness and mysteriousness than their unidentified personal pronouns, the "you" that can be the woman addressed in a love poem or an alter ego or a deity or only the amorphous, unknowable "other" to whom all Celan's poems make their way;

the "he", "she", or "they" that enters a poem without any intro-
duction or identification. Many of these persons may have no
existence or significance outside the poem. It is the poem that
creates them or discovers them. A reader can either relate him-
self to them through his own experience and imagination or he
can not, in which case the "message in the bottle" has not
reached him. If it does reach him it will tell him something of
which he was not aware before reading it. That is the distinction
of poetry like Celan's, poetry always close to the unutterable
because it has passed through it and come out on the other side.

Such poetry demands a special kind of attention and perhaps
a special kind of faith in the authenticity of what it enacts. With-
out the same attention and faith it could not have been written,
for the risk is shared by writer and reader. Speaking about
poetry, Celan quoted this definition by Malebranche: "Attention
is the natural prayer of the soul." I neither know nor consider it
my business to know what Celan believed. It is this quality of
attention in his poems that points to a religious sensibility. The
more we read his poems, the more his kind of attention proves to
be the only adequate response to them.

The present selection from Celan's collections, including the
posthumous ones, still does not encompass the full range of his
work, although I have been able to add considerably to the trans-
lations contained in the earlier *Selected Poems* of 1972 and *Paul
Celan: Poems* of 1980. The German texts in his two-volume
Gedichte, together with those in his last posthumous collection
(which appeared after the two-volume edition), take up more
than 760 pages, and these volumes do not include poems that
Celan left out of his books. Even if I had been capable of trans-
lating all those poems, as I was not, I doubt very much that many
English-speaking readers would have been able to take in such a
large body of unfamiliar work.[3] In the absence of the critical and

[3] The present, enlarged collection of my Celan translations has been
complemented by two books of translations by other hands. They are *65
Poems*, translated by Brian Lynch and Peter Jankowsky, Raven Arts
Press, Dublin, 1985; and *Last Poems*, translated by Katharine Wash-
burn and Margret Guillemin, North Point Press, San Francisco, 1986.

33

annotated edition of Celan's poems that is being prepared, I have picked out a few questions of interpretation as instances of Celan's characteristic procedures, which rest on an extraordinary trust in his readers' capacity to respond to the dominant gesture of a poem without access to the circumstantial data. That trust had to be passed on to his English-speaking readers, though some of them may feel the need to refer to Celan studies in English, like the book by Jerry Glenn, *Paul Celan*, New York, 1973. Any attempt here to provide prose elucidations of all my texts would have swamped the poems themselves in scholarly intricacies and conjectures.

Admittedly, Celan's work becomes most rewarding when read in its entirety; but my own experience is that this reading calls for an application and effort so intense that it may have to be broken off and resumed over the years. Confined though it is to poems that became accessible to me after such repeated readings, this selection should enable readers to feel their way into Celan's work as a whole. Celan is reported to have said: "La poésie ne s'impose plus, elle s'expose", and that is most certainly true of his own later poems. The process of reception, therefore, cannot be other than gradual and slow. It is in the nature of Celan's work that anyone who has opened himself up to that process will be drawn more and more deeply into his enigmas and felicities; and it seems likely that the translation of his work will also have to be done in stages, patiently, for a long time to come.

M. H.
Suffolk, 1979 and 1987

From

Mohn und Gedächtnis

(1952)

TALGLICHT

Die Mönche mit haarigen Fingern schlugen das Buch auf:
   September.
Jason wirft nun mit Schnee nach der aufgegangenen Saat.
Ein Halsband aus Händen gab dir der Wald, so schreitest du tot
   übers Seil.
Ein dunkleres Blau wird zuteil deinem Haar, und ich rede von
   Liebe.
Muscheln red ich und leichtes Gewölk, und ein Boot knospt im
   Regen.
Ein kleiner Hengst jagt über die blätternden Finger –
Schwarz springt das Tor auf, ich singe:
Wie lebten wir hier?

TALLOW LAMP

The monks with hairy fingers opened the book: September.
Now Jason pelts with snow the newly sprouting grain.
The forest gave you a necklace of hands. So dead you walk the
    rope.
To your hair a darker blue is imparted; I speak of love.
Shells I speak and light clouds, and a boat buds in the rain.
A little stallion gallops across the leafing fingers –
Black the gate leaps open, I sing:
How did we live here?

DIE HAND VOLLER STUNDEN, so kamst du zu mir – ich sprach:
Dein Haar ist nicht braun.
So hobst du es leicht auf die Waage des Leids, da war es
   schwerer als ich ...

Sie kommen auf Schiffen zu dir und laden es auf, sie bieten es
   feil auf den Märkten der Lust –
Du lächelst zu mir aus der Tiefe, ich weine zu dir aus der
   Schale, die leicht bleibt.
Ich weine: Dein Haar ist nicht braun, sie bieten das Wasser der
   See, und du gibst ihnen Locken ...
Du flüsterst: Sie füllen die Welt schon mit mir, und ich bleib dir
   ein Hohlweg im Herzen!
Du sagst: Leg das Blattwerk der Jahre zu dir – es ist Zeit, daß du
   kommst und mich küssest!

Das Blattwerk der Jahre ist braun, dein Haar ist es nicht.

YOUR HAND FULL OF HOURS, you came to me – and I said:
Your hair is not brown.
So you lifted it lightly on to the scales of grief; it weighed more
    than I . . .

On ships they come to you and make it their cargo, then put it on
    sale in the markets of lust –
You smile at me from the depth, I weep at you from the scale
    that stays light.
I weep: Your hair is not brown, they offer brine from the sea and
    you give them curls . . .
You whisper: They're filling the world with me now, in your
    heart I'm a hollow way still!
You say: Lay the leafage of years beside you – it's time you came
    closer and kissed me!

The leafage of years is brown, your hair is not brown.

ESPENBAUM, dein Laub blickt weiß ins Dunkel.
Meiner Mutter Haar ward nimmer weiß.

Löwenzahn, so grün ist die Ukraine.
Meine blonde Mutter kam nicht heim.

Regenwolke, säumst du an den Brunnen?
Meine leise Mutter weint für alle.

Runder Stern, du schlingst die goldne Schleife.
Meiner Mutter Herz ward wund von Blei.

Eichne Tür, wer hob dich aus den Angeln?
Meine sanfte Mutter kann nicht kommen.

ASPEN TREE, your leaves glance white into the dark.
My mother's hair was never white.

Dandelion, so green is the Ukraine.
My yellow-haired mother did not come home.

Rain cloud, above the well do you hover?
My quiet mother weeps for everyone.

Round star, you wind the golden loop.
My mother's heart was ripped by lead.

Oaken door, who lifted you off your hinges?
My gentle mother cannot return.

DAS GEHEIMNIS DER FARNE

Im Gewölbe der Schwerter besieht sich der Schatten
    laubgrünes Herz.
Blank sind die Klingen: wer säumte im Tod nicht vor Spiegeln?
Auch wird hier in Krügen kredenzt die lebendige Schwermut:
blumig finstert sie hoch, eh sie trinken, als wär sie nicht Wasser,
als wär sie ein Tausendschön hier, das befragt wird nach
    dunklerer Liebe,
nach schwärzerem Pfühl für das Lager, nach schwererem
    Haar ...

Hier aber wird nur gebangt um den Schimmer des Eisens,
und leuchtet ein Ding hier noch auf, so sei es ein Schwert.
Wir leeren den Krug nur vom Tisch, weil uns Spiegel bewirten:
einer springe entzwei, wo wir grün sind wie Laub!

In the vault of swords the leaf-green heart of the shadows looks
    at itself.
The blades are bright: who would not linger in death before
    mirrors?
Also in jugs here a sadness that's living is drunk to:
flowery it darkens up, before they drink, as though it were not
    water,
as though here it were a daisy of which darker love is demanded,
a pillow more black for the couch, and heavier hair . . .

But here there is only dread for the shining of iron;
and if anything here still glints up, may it be a sword.
Were not mirrors our hosts, never we'd empty the jug from this
    table:
let one of them crack and split where we're green as the leaves.

Schimmelgrün ist das Haus des Vergessens.
Vor jedem der wehenden Tore blaut dein enthaupteter
    Spielmann.
Er schlägt dir die Trommel aus Moos und bitterem Schamhaar;
mit schwärender Zehe malt er im Sand deine Braue.
Länger zeichnet er sie als sie war, und das Rot deiner Lippe.
Du füllst hier die Urnen und speisest dein Herz.

SAND FROM THE URNS

Green as mould is the house of oblivion.
Before each of the blowing gates your beheaded minstrel turns
    blue.
For you he beats his drum made of moss and of harsh pubic hair;
With a festering toe in the sand he traces your eyebrow.
Longer he draws it than ever it was, and the red of your lip.
You fill up the urns here and nourish your heart.

DIE LETZTE FAHNE

Ein wasserfarbenes Wild wird gejagt in den dämmernden
    Marken.
So binde die Maske dir vor und färbe die Wimpern dir grün.
Die Schüssel mit schlummerndem Schrot wird gereicht über
    Ebenholztische:
von Frühling zu Frühling schäumt hier der Wein, so kurz ist das
    Jahr,
so feurig der Preis dieser Schützen – die Rose der Fremde:
dein irrender Bart, die müßige Fahne des Baumstumpfs.

Gewölk und Gebell! Sie reiten den Wahn in den Farn!
Wie Fischer werfen sie Netze nach Irrlicht und Hauch!
Sie schlingen ein Seil um die Kronen und laden zum Tanz!
Und waschen die Hörner im Quell – so lernen sie Lockruf.

Ist dicht, was du wähltest als Mantel, und birgt es den
    Schimmer?
Sie schleichen wie Schlaf um die Stämme, als böten sie Traum.
Die Herzen schleudern sie hoch, die moosigen Bälle des
    Wahnsinns:
o wasserfarbenes Vlies, unser Banner am Turm!

THE LAST FLAG

A water-coloured quarry is chased in the half-light of marches.
So tie on the mask and colour your eyelashes green.
The dish with slumbering shot is served above ebony tables:
from one spring to the next here wine foams, so short is the year,
so fiery the prize of these marksmen – the rose of strange places:
your beard all astray, the tree-stump's indolent banner.

A baying and clouds! Into bracken they're riding their madness!
Like fishermen cast their nets into vapour and will-o'-the-wisp!
They sling a rope round the crests and invite us to dance!
And wash the horns in the wellspring – so learning the lure-call.

What you chose for your cloak, is it dense, can it harbour the
    radiance?
They creep round the trunks like sleep, as though offering
    dream.
High up they hurl hearts, the mossy globes of dementia:
O water-coloured fleece, our one flag on the tower!

EIN KNIRSCHEN VON EISERNEN SCHUHN ist im Kirschbaum.
Aus Helmen schäumt dir der Sommer. Der schwärzliche
  Kuckuck
malt mit demantenem Sporn sein Bild an die Tore des
  Himmels.

Barhaupt ragt aus dem Blattwerk der Reiter.
Im Schild trägt er dämmernd dein Lächeln,
genagelt ans stählerne Schweißtuch des Feindes.
Es ward ihm verheißen der Garten der Träumer,
und Speere hält er bereit, daß die Rose sich ranke ...

Unbeschuht aber kommt durch die Luft, der am meisten dir
  gleichet:
eiserne Schuhe geschnallt an die schmächtigen Hände,
verschläft er die Schlacht und den Sommer. Die Kirsche blutet
  für ihn.

IN THE CHERRY TREE'S BRANCHES a crunching of iron shoes.
Summer foams up for you out of helmets. The blackish cuckoo
with diamond spurs draws his image on to the gates of the sky.

Bareheaded the horseman looms up from the foliage.
On his shield he bears the dusk of your smile,
nailed on to the enemy's kerchief of steel.
The garden of dreamers was promised to him,
and spears he keeps ready, so that the rose will climb ...

But unshod through the air comes he who resembles you most:
iron shoes buckled on to his delicate hands,
he sleeps through the battle and summer. It's for him that the
    cherry bleeds.

DAS GASTMAHL

Geleert sei die Nacht aus den Flaschen im hohen Gebälk der
    Versuchung,
die Schwelle mit Zähnen gepflügt, vor Morgen der Jähzorn
    gesät:
es schießt wohl empor uns ein Moos noch, eh von der Mühle sie
    hier sind,
ein leises Getreide zu finden bei uns ihrem langsamen Rad ...

Unter den giftigen Himmeln sind andere Halme wohl falber,
wird anders der Traum noch gemünzt als hier, wo wir würfeln
    um Lust,
als hier, wo getauscht wird im Dunkel Vergessen und Wunder,
wo alles nur gilt eine Stunde und schwelgend bespien wird von
    uns,
ins gierige Wasser der Fenster geschleudert in leuchtenden
    Truhen –:
es birst auf der Straße der Menschen, den Wolken zum Ruhm!

So hüllet euch denn in die Mäntel und steiget mit mir auf die
    Tische:
wie anders sei noch geschlafen als stehend, inmitten der Kelche?
Wem trinken wir Träume noch zu, als dem langsamen Rad?

Let the night be drained from the flasks in temptation's high
    rafters,
the threshold be ploughed with teeth, before morning quick fury
    be sown:
a moss may shoot up for us here before from the mill they
have come in search of a quiet grain for their sluggish wheel . . .

Under the venomous skies there must be more yellowish
    cornstalks,
and differently dream is minted than here where for pleasure we
    cast the dice,
than here where in darkness oblivion and wonder are bartered,
where for one hour a thing counts and is spewed on by us in our
    revels,
at the greedy water of windows flung down in luminous
    coffers —:
it bursts on the pavement of men, to the glory of clouds.

Then wrap yourselves in your cloaks and join me in climbing the
    tables:
how else shall anyone sleep but standing, with chalices round
    him?
To whom do we still drink our dreams if not to the sluggish
    wheel?

ERINNERUNG AN FRANKREICH

Du denk mit mir: der Himmel von Paris, die große
    Herbstzeitlose . . .
Wir kauften Herzen bei den Blumenmädchen:
sie waren blau und blühten auf im Wasser.
Es fing zu regnen an in unserer Stube,
und unser Nachbar kam, Monsieur Le Songe, ein hager
    Männlein.
Wir spielten Karten, ich verlor die Augensterne;
du liehst dein Haar mir, ich verlors, er schlug uns nieder.
Er trat zur Tür hinaus, der Regen folgt' ihm.
Wir waren tot und konnten atmen.

Together with me recall: the sky of Paris, that giant autumn
    crocus . . .
We went shopping for hearts at the flower girl's booth:
they were blue and they opened up in the water.
It began to rain in our room,
and our neighbour came in, Monsieur Le Songe, a lean little
    man.
We played cards, I lost the irises of my eyes;
you lent me your hair, I lost it, he struck us down.
He left by the door, the rain followed him out.
We were dead and were able to breathe.

CHANSON EINER DAME IM SCHATTEN

Wenn die Schweigsame kommt und die Tulpen köpft:
Wer gewinnt?
        Wer verliert?
                Wer tritt an das Fenster?
Wer nennt ihren Namen zuerst?

Es ist einer, der trägt mein Haar.
Er trägts wie man Tote trägt auf den Händen.
Er trägts wie der Himmel mein Haar trug im Jahr, da ich liebte.
Er trägt es aus Eitelkeit so.

Der gewinnt.
        Der verliert nicht.
                Der tritt nicht ans Fenster.
Der nennt ihren Namen nicht.

Es ist einer, der hat meine Augen.
Er hat sie, seit Tore sich schließen.
Er trägt sie am Finger wie Ringe.
Er trägt sie wie Scherben von Lust und Saphir:
er war schon mein Bruder im Herbst;
er zählt schon die Tage und Nächte.

Der gewinnt.
        Der verliert nicht.
                Der tritt nicht ans Fenster.
Der nennt ihren Namen zuletzt.

Es ist einer, der hat, was ich sagte.
Er trägts unterm Arm wie ein Bündel.
Er trägts wie die Uhr ihre schlechteste Stunde.
Er trägt es von Schwelle zu Schwelle, er wirft es nicht fort.

CHANSON OF A LADY IN THE SHADE

When the silent one comes and beheads the tulips:
Who wins?
       Who loses?
               Who walks to the window?
Who's the first to speak her name?

He is one who wears my hair.
He wears it much as one wears the dead on one's hands.
He wears it much as the sky wore my hair that year when I loved.
He wears it like that out of vanity.

That one wins.
       Doesn't lose.
               Doesn't walk to the window.
He does not speak her name.

He is one who has my eyes.
He's had them since gates have shut.
He wears them like rings on his fingers.
He wears them like shards of sapphire and lust:
since the autumn he has been my brother;
he's counting the days and the nights.

That one wins.
       Doesn't lose.
               Doesn't walk to the window.
He's the last to speak her name.

He's one who has what I said.
He carries it under his arm like a bundle.
He carries it as the clock carries its worst hour.
From threshold to threshold he carries it, never throws it away.

Der gewinnt nicht.
Der verliert.
Der tritt an das Fenster.
Der nennt ihren Namen zuerst.

Der wird mit den Tulpen geköpft.

NACHTSTRAHL

Am lichtesten brannte das Haar meiner Abendgeliebten:
ihr schick ich den Sarg aus dem leichtesten Holz.
Er ist wellenumwogt wie das Bett unsrer Träume in Rom;
er trägt eine weiße Perücke wie ich und spricht heiser:
er redet wie ich, wenn ich Einlaß gewähre den Herzen.
Er weiß ein französisches Lied von der Liebe, das sang ich im
     Herbst,
als ich weilte auf Reisen in Spätland und Briefe schrieb an den
     Morgen.

Ein schöner Kahn ist der Sarg, geschnitzt im Gehölz der
     Gefühle.
Auch ich fuhr blutabwärts mit ihm, als ich jünger war als dein
     Aug.
Nun bist du jung wie ein toter Vogel im Märzschnee,
nun kommt er zu dir und singt sein französisches Lied.
Ihr seid leicht: ihr schlaft meinen Frühling zu Ende.
Ich bin leichter:
ich singe vor Fremden.

That one doesn't win.
        He loses.
                He walks to the window.
He's the first to speak her name.

With the tulips that one's beheaded.

NIGHT RAY

Most brightly of all burned the hair of my evening loved one:
to her I send the coffin of lightest wood.
Waves billow round it as round the bed of our dream in Rome;
it wears a white wig as I do and speaks hoarsely:
it talks as I do when I grant admittance to hearts.
It knows a French song about love, I sang it in autumn
when I stopped as a tourist in Lateland and wrote my letters to
      morning.

A fine boat is that coffin carved in the coppice of feelings.
I too drift in it downbloodstream, younger still than your eye.
Now you are young as a bird dropped dead in March snow,
now it comes to you, sings you its love song from France.
You are light: you will sleep through my spring till it's over.
I am lighter:
in front of strangers I sing.

DIE JAHRE VON DIR ZU MIR

Wieder wellt sich dein Haar, wenn ich wein. Mit dem Blau
    deiner Augen
deckst du den Tisch unsrer Liebe: ein Bett zwischen Sommer
    und Herbst.
Wir trinken, was einer gebraut, der nicht ich war, noch du, noch
    ein dritter:
wir schlürfen ein Leeres und Letztes.

Wir sehen uns zu in den Spiegeln der Tiefsee und reichen uns
    rascher die Speisen:
die Nacht ist die Nacht, sie beginnt mit dem Morgen,
sie legt mich zu dir.

THE YEARS FROM YOU TO ME

Your hair waves once more when I weep. With the blue of your
    eyes
you lay the table of love: a bed between summer and autumn.
We drink what somebody brewed, neither I nor you nor a third:
we lap up some empty and last thing.

We watch ourselves in the deep sea's mirrors and faster pass
    food to the other:
the night is the night, it begins with the morning,
beside you it lays me down.

CORONA

Aus der Hand frißt der Herbst mir sein Blatt: wir sind Freunde.
Wir schälen die Zeit aus den Nüssen und lehren sie gehn:
die Zeit kehrt zurück in die Schale.

Im Spiegel ist Sonntag,
im Traum wird geschlafen,
der Mund redet wahr.

Mein Aug steigt hinab zum Geschlecht der Geliebten:
wir sehen uns an,
wir sagen uns Dunkles,
wir lieben einander wie Mohn und Gedächtnis,
wir schlafen wie Wein in den Muscheln,
wie das Meer im Blutstrahl des Mondes.

Wir stehen umschlungen im Fenster, sie sehen uns zu von der
    Straße:
es ist Zeit, daß man weiß!
Es ist Zeit, daß der Stein sich zu blühen bequemt,
daß der Unrast ein Herz schlägt.
Es ist Zeit, daß es Zeit wird.

Es ist Zeit.

Autumn eats its leaf out of my hand: we are friends.
From the nuts we shell time and we teach it to walk:
then time returns to the shell.

In the mirror it's Sunday,
in dream there is room for sleeping,
our mouths speak the truth.

My eye moves down to the sex of my loved one:
we look at each other,
we exchange dark words,
we love each other like poppy and recollection,
we sleep like wine in the conches,
like the sea in the moon's blood ray.

We stand by the window embracing, and people look up from
    the street:
it is time they knew!
It is time the stone made an effort to flower,
time unrest had a beating heart.
It is time it were time.

It is time.

TODESFUGE

Schwarze Milch der Frühe wir trinken sie abends
wir trinken sie mittags und morgens wir trinken sie nachts
wir trinken und trinken
wir schaufeln ein Grab in den Lüften da liegt man nicht eng
Ein Mann wohnt im Haus der spielt mit den Schlangen der
    schreibt
der schreibt wenn es dunkelt nach Deutschland dein goldenes
    Haar Margarete
er schreibt es und tritt vor das Haus und es blitzen die Sterne er
    pfeift seine Rüden herbei
er pfeift seine Juden hervor läßt schaufeln ein Grab in der Erde
er befiehlt uns spielt auf nun zum Tanz

Schwarze Milch der Frühe wir trinken dich nachts
wir trinken dich morgens und mittags wir trinken dich abends
wir trinken und trinken
Ein Mann wohnt im Haus der spielt mit den Schlangen der
    schreibt
der schreibt wenn es dunkelt nach Deutschland dein goldenes
    Haar Margarete
Dein aschenes Haar Sulamith wir schaufeln ein Grab in den
    Lüften da liegt man nicht eng

Er ruft stecht tiefer ins Erdreich ihr einen ihr andern singet und
    spielt
er greift nach dem Eisen im Gurt er schwingts seine Augen sind
    blau
stecht tiefer die Spaten ihr einen ihr andern spielt weiter zum
    Tanz auf

Schwarze Milch der Frühe wir trinken dich nachts
wir trinken dich mittags und morgens wir trinken dich abends
wir trinken und trinken
ein Mann wohnt im Haus dein goldenes Haar Margarete
dein aschenes Haar Sulamith er spielt mit den Schlangen

DEATH FUGUE

Black milk of daybreak we drink it at sundown
we drink it at noon in the morning we drink it at night
we drink and we drink it
we dig a grave in the breezes there one lies unconfined
A man lives in the house he plays with the serpents he writes
he writes when dusk falls to Germany your golden hair
    Margarete
he writes it and steps out of doors and the stars are flashing he
    whistles his pack out
he whistles his Jews out in earth has them dig for a grave
he commands us strike up for the dance

Black milk of daybreak we drink you at night
we drink in the morning at noon we drink you at sundown
we drink and we drink you
A man lives in the house he plays with the serpents he writes
he writes when dusk falls to Germany your golden hair
    Margarete
your ashen hair Shulamith we dig a grave in the breezes there
    one lies unconfined

He calls out jab deeper into the earth you lot you others sing now
    and play
he grabs at the iron in his belt he waves it his eyes are blue
jab deeper you lot with your spades you others play on for the
    dance

Black milk of daybreak we drink you at night
we drink you at noon in the morning we drink you at sundown
we drink and we drink you
a man lives in the house your golden hair Margarete
your ashen hair Shulamith he plays with the serpents

Er ruft spielt süßer den Tod der Tod ist ein Meister aus
   Deutschland
er ruft streicht dunkler die Geigen dann steigt ihr als Rauch in
   die Luft
dann habt ihr ein Grab in den Wolken da liegt man nicht eng

Schwarze Milch der Frühe wir trinken dich nachts
wir trinken dich mittags der Tod ist ein Meister aus
   Deutschland
wir trinken dich abends und morgens wir trinken und trinken
der Tod ist ein Meister aus Deutschland sein Auge ist blau
er trifft dich mit bleierner Kugel er trifft dich genau
ein Mann wohnt im Haus dein goldenes Haar Margarete
er hetzt seine Rüden auf uns er schenkt uns ein Grab in der Luft
er spielt mit den Schlangen und träumet der Tod ist ein Meister
   aus Deutschland

dein goldenes Haar Margarete
dein aschenes Haar Sulamith

He calls out more sweetly play death death is a master from
    Germany
he calls out more darkly now stroke your strings then as smoke
    you will rise into air
then a grave you will have in the clouds there one lies unconfined

Black milk of daybreak we drink you at night
we drink you at noon death is a master from Germany
we drink you at sundown and in the morning we drink and we
    drink you
death is a master from Germany his eyes are blue
he strikes you with leaden bullets his aim is true
a man lives in the house your golden hair Margarete
he sets his pack on to us he grants us a grave in the air
he plays with the serpents and daydreams death is a master from
    Germany

your golden hair Margarete
your ashen hair Shulamith

INS NEBELHORN

Mund im verborgenen Spiegel,
Knie vor der Säule des Hochmuts,
Hand mit dem Gitterstab:

reicht euch das Dunkel,
nennt meinen Namen,
führt mich vor ihn.

VOM BLAU, das noch sein Auge sucht, trink ich als erster.
Aus deiner Fußspur trink ich und ich seh:
du rollst mir durch die Finger, Perle, und du wächst!
Du wächst wie alle, die vergessen sind.
Du rollst: das schwarze Hagelkorn der Schwermut
fällt in ein Tuch, ganz weiß vom Abschiedwinken.

INTO THE FOGHORN

Mouth in the hidden mirror,
knee at the pillar of pride,
hand with the bar of a cage:

proffer yourselves the dark,
speak my name,
lead me to him.

I AM THE FIRST to drink of the blue that still looks for its eye.
I drink from your footprint and see:
you roll through my fingers, pearl, and you grow!
You grow, as do all the forgotten.
You roll: the black hailstone of sadness
is caught by a kerchief turned white with waving goodbye.

KRISTALL

Nicht an meinen Lippen suche deinen Mund,
nicht vorm Tor den Fremdling,
nicht im Aug die Träne.

Sieben Nächte höher wandert Rot zu Rot,
sieben Herzen tiefer pocht die Hand ans Tor,
sieben Rosen später rauscht der Brunnen.

CRYSTAL

Not on my lips look for your mouth,
not in front of the gate for the stranger,
not in the eye for the tear.

Seven nights higher red makes for red,
seven hearts deeper the hand knocks on the gate,
seven roses later plashes the fountain.

TOTENHEMD

Was du aus Leichtem wobst,
trag ich dem Stein zu Ehren.
Wenn ich im Dunkel die Schreie
wecke, weht es sie an.

Oft, wenn ich stammeln soll,
wirft es vergessene Falten,
und der ich bin, verzeiht
dem, der ich war.

Aber der Haldengott
rührt seine dumpfeste Trommel,
und wie die Falte fiel,
runzelt der Finstre die Stirn.

SHROUD

That which you wove out of light thread
I wear in honour of stone.
When in the dark I awaken
the screams, it blows on them, lightly.

Often, when I should stammer,
it raises forgotten crinkles
and he that I am forgives
him that I was.

But the god of the slagheaps
beats his most muted drum,
and just as the crinkle ran
the grim one puckers his brow.

DER REISEKAMERAD

Deiner Mutter Seele schwebt voraus.
Deiner Mutter Seele hilft die Nacht umschiffen, Riff um Riff.
Deiner Mutter Seele peitscht die Haie vor dir her.

Dieses Wort ist deiner Mutter Mündel.
Deiner Mutter Mündel teilt dein Lager, Stein um Stein.
Deiner Mutter Mündel bückt sich nach der Krume Lichts.

THE TRAVELLING COMPANION

Your mother's soul hovers ahead.
Your mother's soul helps to navigate night, reef after reef.
Your mother's soul whips on the sharks at the bow.

This word is your mother's ward.
Your mother's ward shares your couch, stone by stone.
Your mother's ward stoops for the crumb of light.

AUGEN:
schimmernd vom Regen, der strömte,
als Gott mir zu trinken befahl.

Augen:
Gold, das die Nacht in die Hände mir zählt',
als ich Nesseln pflückt'
und die Schatten der Sprüche reutet'.

Augen:
Abend, der über mir aufglomm, als ich aufriß das Tor
und durchwintert vom Eis meiner Schläfen
durch die Weiler der Ewigkeit sprengt'.

LANDSCHAFT

Ihr hohen Pappeln – Menschen dieser Erde!
Ihr schwarzen Teiche Glücks – ihr spiegelt sie zu Tode!

Ich sah dich, Schwester, stehn in diesem Glanze.

EYES:
shining with the rain that poured
when God bade me drink.

Eyes:
gold that night counted into my hands
when I gathered nettles
and hoed the shadows of proverbs.

Eyes:
evening, kindled above me when I tore open the gate
and wintered right through by the ice of my temples,
I galloped on through eternity's hamlets.

LANDSCAPE

Tall poplars – human beings of this earth!
Black ponds of happiness – you mirror them to death!

I saw you, sister, stand in that effulgence.

ZÄHLE die Mandeln,
zähle, was bitter war und dich wachhielt,
zähl mich dazu:

Ich suchte dein Aug, als du's aufschlugst und niemand dich
    ansah,
ich spann jenen heimlichen Faden,
an dem der Tau, den du dachtest,
hinunterglitt zu den Krügen,
die ein Spruch, der zu niemandes Herz fand, behütet.

Dort erst tratest du ganz in den Namen, der dein ist,
schrittest du sicheren Fußes zu dir,
schwangen die Hämmer frei im Glockenstuhl deines
    Schweigens,
stieß das Erlauschte zu dir,
legte das Tote den Arm auch um dich,
und ihr ginget selbdritt durch den Abend.

Mache mich bitter.
Zähle mich zu den Mandeln.

COUNT the almonds,
count what was bitter and kept you awake,
count me in:

I looked for your eye when you opened it, no one was looking at
    you,
I spun that secret thread
on which the dew you were thinking
slid down to the jugs
guarded by words that to no one's heart found their way.

Only there did you wholly enter the name that is yours,
sure-footed stepped into yourself,
freely the hammers swung in the bell frame of your silence,
the listened for reached you,
what is dead put its arm round you also
and the three of you walked through the evening.

Make me bitter.
Count me among the almonds.

FROM
Von Schwelle zu Schwelle
(1955)

VON DUNKEL ZU DUNKEL

Du schlugst die Augen auf – ich seh mein Dunkel leben.
Ich seh ihm auf den Grund:
auch da ists mein und lebt.

Setzt solches über? Und erwacht dabei?
Wes Licht folgt auf dem Fuß mir,
daß sich ein Ferge fand?

GRABSCHRIFT FÜR FRANÇOIS

Die beiden Türen der Welt
stehen offen:
geöffnet von dir
in der Zwienacht.
Wir hören sie schlagen und schlagen
und tragen das ungewisse,
und tragen das Grün in dein Immer.

Oktober 1953

FROM DARKNESS TO DARKNESS

You opened your eyes – I saw my darkness live.
I see through it down to the bed:
there too it is mine and lives.

Is that a ferry? Which, crossing, awakens?
Whose light can it be at my heels
for a boatman to appear?

EPITAPH FOR FRANÇOIS

The two doors of the world
stand open:
opened by you
in the twinight.
We hear them slam and slam
and carry the thing that's uncertain
and carry the green thing into your Ever.

October 1953

Umbrische Nacht.
Umbrische Nacht mit dem Silber von Glocke und Ölblatt.
Umbrische Nacht mit dem Stein, den du hertrugst.
Umbrische Nacht mit dem Stein.

    Stumm, was ins Leben stieg, stumm.
    Füll die Krüge um.

Irdener Krug.
Irdener Krug, dran die Töpferhand festwuchs.
Irdener Krug, den die Hand eines Schattens für immer
   verschloß.
Irdener Krug mit dem Siegel des Schattens.

    Stein, wo du hinsiehst, Stein.
    Laß das Grautier ein.

Trottendes Tier.
Trottendes Tier im Schnee, den die nackteste Hand streut.
Trottendes Tier vor dem Wort, das ins Schloß fiel.
Trottendes Tier, das den Schlaf aus der Hand frißt.

    Glanz, der nicht trösten will, Glanz.
    Die Toten – sie betteln noch, Franz.

Umbrian night.
Umbrian night with the silver of churchbell and olive leaf.
Umbrian night with the stone that you carried here.
Umbrian night with the stone.

Dumb, that which rose into life, dumb.
Refill the jugs, come.

Earthenware jug.
Earthenware jug to which the potter's hand grew affixed.
Earthenware jug which a shade's hand closed for ever.
Earthenware jug with a shade's seal.

Stone, wherever you look, stone.
Let the grey animal in.

Trotting animal.
Trotting animal in the snow the nakedest hand scatters.
Trotting animal before the word that clicked shut.
Trotting animal that takes sleep from the feeding hand.

Brightness that will not comfort, brightness you shed.
Still they are begging, Francis – the dead.

AUCH HEUTE ABEND

Voller,
da Schnee auch auf dieses
sonnendurchschwommene Meer fiel,
blüht das Eis in den Körben,
die du zur Stadt trägst.

Sand
heischst du dafür,
denn die letzte
Rose daheim
will auch heut abend gespeist sein
aus rieselnder Stunde.

THIS EVENING ALSO

More fully,
since snow fell even on this
sun-drifted, sun-drenched sea,
blossoms the ice in those baskets
you carry into town.

Sand
you demand in return,
for the last
rose back at home
this evening also wants to be fed
out of the trickling hour.

VOR EINER KERZE

Aus getriebenem Golde, so
wie du's mir anbefahlst, Mutter,
formt ich den Leuchter, daraus
sie empor mir dunkelt inmitten
splitternder Stunden:
deines
Totseins Tochter.

Schlank von Gestalt,
ein schmaler, mandeläugiger Schatten,
Mund und Geschlecht
umtanzt von Schlummergetier,
entschwebt sie dem klaffenden Golde,
steigt sie hinan
zum Scheitel des Jetzt.

Mit nachtverhangnen
Lippen
sprech ich den Segen:

    Im Namen der Drei,
    die einander befehden, bis
    der Himmel hinabtaucht ins Grab der Gefühle,
    im Namen der Drei, deren Ringe
    am Finger mir glänzen, sooft
    ich den Bäumen im Abgrund das Haar lös,
    auf daß die Tiefe durchrauscht sei von reicherer Flut –,
    im Namen des ersten der Drei,
    der aufschrie,
    als es zu leben galt dort, wo vor ihm sein Wort schon
        gewesen,
    im Namen des zweiten, der zusah und weinte,
    im Namen des dritten, der weiße
    Steine häuft in der Mitte, –
    sprech ich dich frei
    vom Amen, das uns übertäubt,

IN FRONT OF A CANDLE

Of chased gold, as
you instructed me, Mother,
I shaped the candlestick from which
she darkens up for me in the midst
of splintering hours:
your
being dead's daughter.

Slender in build,
a narrow, almond-eyed shade,
her mouth and her sex
surrounded by slumber beasts, dancing,
she drifts up from the gaping gold,
she ascends
to the crown of the Now.

With lips draped
by night
I speak the blessing:

 In the name of the three
 who war among themselves until
 heaven dips down into the grave of feelings,
 in the name of the three whose rings
 glint on my finger whenever
 I loosen the hair of the trees in the chasm,
 so that richer torrents may rush through the deeps –,
 in the name of the first of the three,
 who cried out
 when called upon to live where his word had been before
  him,
 in the name of the second who looked on and wept,
 in the name of the third, who piles up
 white stones in the centre, –
 I pronounce you free
 of the amen that drowns our voices,

vom eisigen Licht, das es säumt,
da, wo es turmhoch ins Meer tritt,
da, wo die graue, die Taube
aufpickt die Namen
diesseits und jenseits des Sterbens:
Du bleibst, du bleibst, du bleibst
einer Toten Kind,
geweiht dem Nein meiner Sehnsucht,
vermählt einer Schrunde der Zeit,
vor die mich das Mutterwort führte,
auf daß ein einziges Mal·
erzittre die Hand,
die je und je mir ans Herz greift!

of the icy light on its edges
where, high as a tower, it enters the sea,
where the grey one, the dove
pecks up the names
on this and the other side of dying:
you remain, you remain, you remain
a dead woman's child,
to the No of my longing consecrated,
wedded to a fissure in time
to which I was led by a mother's word
so that once only
a tremor should pass through the hand
that again and again reaches out for my heart.

MIT WECHSELNDEM SCHLÜSSEL

Mit wechselndem Schlüssel
schließt du das Haus auf, darin
der Schnee des Verschwiegenen treibt.
Je nach dem Blut, das dir quillt
aus Aug oder Mund oder Ohr,
wechselt dein Schlüssel.

Wechselt dein Schlüssel, wechselt das Wort,
das treiben darf mit den Flocken.
Je nach dem Wind, der dich fortstößt,
ballt um das Wort sich der Schnee.

With a variable key
you unlock the house in which
drifts the snow of that left unspoken.
Always what key you choose
depends on the blood that spurts
from your eye or your mouth or your ear.

You vary the key, you vary the word
that is free to drift with the flakes.
What snowball will form round the word
depends on the wind that rebuffs you.

NÄCHTLICH GESCHÜRZT

Für Hannah und Hermann Lenz

Nächtlich geschürzt
die Lippen der Blumen,
gekreuzt und verschränkt
die Schäfte der Fichten,
ergraut das Moos, erschüttert der Stein,
erwacht zum unendlichen Fluge
die Dohlen über dem Gletscher:

dies ist die Gegend, wo
rasten, die wir ereilt:

sie werden die Stunde nicht nennen,
die Flocken nicht zählen,
den Wassern nicht folgen ans Wehr.

Sie stehen getrennt in der Welt,
ein jeglicher bei seiner Nacht,
ein jeglicher bei seinem Tode,
unwirsch, barhaupt, bereift
von Nahem und Fernem.

Sie tragen die Schuld ab, die ihren Ursprung beseelte,
sie tragen sie ab an ein Wort,
das zu Unrecht besteht, wie der Sommer.

Ein Wort – du weißt:
eine Leiche.

Laß uns sie waschen,
laß uns sie kämmen,
laß uns ihr Aug
himmelwärts wenden.

NOCTURNALLY POUTING

For Hannah and Hermann Lenz

Nocturnally pouting
the lips of flowers,
criss-crossed and linked
the shafts of the spruces,
turned grey the moss, the stone shaken,
roused for unending flight
the jackdaws over the glacier:

this is the region where
those we've caught up with rest:

they will not name the hour,
they will not count the flakes
nor follow the stream to the weir.

They stand apart in the world,
each one close up to his night,
each one close up to his death,
surly, bare-headed, hoar-frosted
with all that is near, all that's far.

They discharge the guilt that adhered to their origin,
they discharge it upon a word
that wrongly subsists, like summer.

A word – you know:
a corpse.

Let us wash it,
let us comb it,
let us turn its eye
towards heaven.

AUGE DER ZEIT

Dies ist das Auge der Zeit:
es blickt scheel
unter siebenfarbener Braue.
Sein Lid wird von Feuern gewaschen,
seine Träne ist Dampf.

Der blinde Stern fliegt es an
und zerschmilzt an der heißeren Wimper:
es wird warm in der Welt,
und die Toten
knospen und blühen.

TIME'S EYE

This is time's eye:
it squints out
from under a seven-hued eyebrow.
Its lid is washed clean by fires,
its tear is hot steam.

Towards it the blind star flies
and melts at the eyelash that's hotter:
it's growing warm in the world
and the dead
burgeon and flower.

IN MEMORIAM PAUL ELUARD

Lege dem Toten die Worte ins Grab,
die er sprach, um zu leben.
Bette sein Haupt zwischen sie,
laß ihn fühlen
die Zungen der Sehnsucht,
die Zangen.

Leg auf die Lider des Toten das Wort,
das er jenem verweigert,
der du zu ihm sagte,
das Wort,
an dem das Blut seines Herzens vorbeisprang,
als eine Hand, so nackt wie die seine,
jenen, der du zu ihm sagte,
in die Bäume der Zukunft knüpfte.

Leg ihm dies Wort auf die Lider:
vielleicht
tritt in sein Aug, das noch blau ist,
eine zweite, fremdere Bläue,
und jener, der du zu ihm sagte,
träumt mit ihm: Wir.

IN MEMORIAM PAUL ELUARD

Lay those words into the dead man's grave
which he spoke in order to live.
Pillow his head amid them,
let him feel
the tongues of longing,
the tongs.

Lay that word on the dead man's eyelids
which he refused to him
who addressed him as thou,
the word
his leaping heart-blood passed by
when a hand as bare as his own
knotted him who addressed him as thou
into the trees of the future.

Lay this word on his eyelids:
perhaps
his eye, still blue, will assume
a second, more alien blueness,
and he who addressed him as thou
will dream with him: We.

Mitsamt meinen Steinen,
den großgeweinten
hinter den Gittern,

schleiften sie mich
in die Mitte des Marktes,
dorthin,
wo die Fahne sich aufrollt, der ich
keinerlei Eid schwor.

Flöte,
Doppelflöte der Nacht:
denke der dunklen
Zwillingsröte
in Wien und Madrid.

Setz deine Fahne auf Halbmast,
Erinnrung.
Auf Halbmast
für heute und immer.

Herz:
gib dich auch hier zu erkennen,
hier, in der Mitte des Marktes.
Ruf's, das Schibboleth, hinaus
in die Fremde der Heimat:
Februar. No pasaran.

Einhorn:
du weißt um die Steine,
du weißt um die Wasser,
komm,
ich führ dich hinweg
zu den Stimmen
von Estremadura.

SHIBBOLETH

Together with my stones
grown big with weeping
behind the bars,

they dragged me out into
the middle of the market,
that place
where the flag unfurls to which
I swore no kind of allegiance.

Flute,
double flute of night:
remember the dark
twin redness
of Vienna and Madrid.

Set your flag at half-mast,
memory.
At half-mast
today and for ever.

Heart:
here too reveal what you are,
here, in the midst of the market.
Call the shibboleth, call it out
into your alien homeland:
February. *No pasarán*.

Unicorn:
you know about the stones,
you know about the water,
come,
I shall lead you away
to the voices
of Estremadura.

SPRICH AUCH DU

Sprich auch du,
sprich als letzter,
sag deinen Spruch.

Sprich –
Doch scheide das Nein nicht vom Ja.
Gib deinem Spruch auch den Sinn:
gib ihm den Schatten.

Gib ihm Schatten genug,
gib ihm so viel,
also du um dich verteilt weißt zwischen
Mittnacht und Mittag und Mittnacht.

Blicke umher:
sieh, wie's lebendig wird rings –
Beim Tode! Lebendig!
Wahr spricht, wer Schatten spricht.

Nun aber schrumpft der Ort, wo du stehst:
Wohin jetzt, Schattenentblößter, wohin?
Steige. Taste empor.
Dünner wirst du, unkenntlicher, feiner!
Feiner: ein Faden,
an dem er herabwill, der Stern:
um unten zu schwimmen, unten,
wo er sich schimmern sieht: in der Dünung
wandernder Worte.

SPEAK, YOU ALSO

Speak, you also,
speak as the last,
have your say.

Speak –
But keep yes and no unsplit.
And give your say this meaning:
give it the shade.

Give it shade enough,
give it as much
as you know has been dealt out between
midnight and midday and midnight.

Look around:
look how it all leaps alive –
where death is! Alive!
He speaks truly who speaks the shade.

But now shrinks the place where you stand:
Where now, stripped by shade, will you go?
Upward. Grope your way up.
Thinner you grow, less knowable, finer.
Finer: a thread by which
it wants to be lowered, the star:
to float farther down, down below
where it sees itself gleam: in the swell
of wandering words.

INSELHIN

Inselhin, neben den Toten,
dem Einbaum waldher vermählt,
von Himmeln umgeiert die Arme,
die Seelen saturnisch beringt:

so rudern die Fremden und Freien,
die Meister vom Eis und vom Stein:
umläutet von sinkenden Bojen,
umbellt von der haiblauen See.

Sie rudern, sie rudern, sie rudern –:
Ihr Toten, ihr Schwimmer, voraus!
Umgittert auch dies von der Reuse!
Und morgen verdampft unser Meer!

ISLEWARD

Isleward, next to the dead,
wedded from woods to the dugout,
their arms vultured round with skies,
their souls saturninely ringed:

so the foreign, the free ones row,
the masters of ice and of stone:
chimed at by sinking buoys,
barked at by shark-blue ocean.

They row, they row, they row –:
You dead, you swimmers, lead on!
This, too, surround with the bow-net!
And tomorrow our sea will be dry!

FROM
Sprachgitter
(1959)

ZUVERSICHT

Es wird noch ein Aug sein,
ein fremdes, neben
dem unsern: stumm
unter steinernem Lid.

Kommt, bohrt euren Stollen!

Es wird eine Wimper sein,
einwärts gekehrt im Gestein,
von Ungeweintem verstählt,
die feinste der Spindeln.

Vor euch tut sie das Werk,
als gäb es, weil Stein ist, noch Brüder.

CONFIDENCE

There will be another eye,
a strange one, beside
our own: unspeaking
under its stony lid.

Come, drill your adits!

There will be an eyelash,
turned inward in the rock,
steeled by what was not wept,
the finest of spindles.

Before you it does the work, as though,
because stone is, still there were brothers.

MIT BRIEF UND UHR

Wachs,
Ungeschriebnes zu siegeln,
das deinen Namen
erriet,
das deinen Namen
verschlüsselt.

Kommst du nun, schwimmendes Licht?

Finger, wächsern auch sie,
durch fremde,
schmerzende Ringe gezogen.
Fortgeschmolzen die Kuppen.

Kommst du, schwimmendes Licht?

Zeitleer die Waben der Uhr,
bräutlich das Immentausend,
reisebereit.

Komm, schwimmendes Licht.

UNTER EIN BILD

Rabenüberschwärmte Weizenwoge.
Welchen Himmels Blau? Des untern? Obern?
Später Pfeil, der von der Seele schnellte.
Stärkres Schwirren. Näh'res Glühen. Beide Welten.

WITH LETTER AND CLOCK

Wax
to seal the unwritten
that guessed
your name,
that enciphers
your name.

Swimming light, will you come now?

Fingers, waxen too,
drawn
through strange, painful rings.
The tips melted away.

Swimming light, will you come?

Empty of time the honeycomb cells of the clock,
bridal the thousand of bees,
ready to leave.

Swimming light, come.

UNDER A PICTURE

Swarming of ravens over a wheat billow.
Blue of which heaven? The higher? Nether?
Late arrow that the soul released.
Louder whirring. Nearer glow. This world *and* the other.

HEIMKEHR

Schneefall, dichter und dichter,
taubenfarben, wie gestern,
Schneefall, als schliefst du auch jetzt noch.

Weithin gelagertes Weiß.
Drüberhin, endlos,
die Schlittenspur des Verlornen.

Darunter, geborgen,
stülpt sich empor,
was den Augen so weh tut,
Hügel um Hügel,
unsichtbar.

Auf jedem,
heimgeholt in sein Heute,
ein ins Stumme entglittenes Ich:
hölzern, ein Pflock.

Dort: ein Gefühl,
vom Eiswind herübergeweht,
das sein tauben-, sein schnee-
farbenes Fahnentuch festmacht.

HOMECOMING

Snowfall, denser and denser,
dove-coloured as yesterday,
snowfall, as if even now you were sleeping.

White, stacked into distance.
Above it, endless,
the sleigh track of the lost.

Below, hidden,
presses up
what so hurts the eyes,
hill upon hill,
invisible.

On each,
fetched home into its today,
an I slipped away into dumbness:
wooden, a post.

There: a feeling,
blown across by the ice wind
attaching its dove- its snow-
coloured cloth as a flag.

UNTEN

Heimgeführt ins Vergessen
das Gast-Gespräch unsrer
langsamen Augen.

Heimgeführt Silbe um Silbe, verteilt
auf die tagblinden Würfel, nach denen
die spielende Hand greift, groß,
im Erwachen.

Und das Zuviel meiner Rede:
angelagert dem kleinen
Kristall in der Tracht deines Schweigens.

BELOW

Led home into oblivion
the sociable talk of
our slow eyes.

Led home, syllable after syllable, shared
out among the dayblind dice, for which
the playing hand reaches out, large,
awakening.

And the too much of my speaking:
heaped up round the little
crystal dressed in the style of your silence.

TENEBRAE

Nah sind wir, Herr,
nahe und greifbar.

Gegriffen schon, Herr,
ineinander verkrallt, als wär
der Leib eines jeden von uns
dein Leib, Herr.

Bete, Herr,
bete zu uns,
wir sind nah.

Windschief gingen wir hin,
gingen wir hin, uns zu bücken
nach Mulde und Maar.

Zur Tränke gingen wir, Herr.

Es war Blut, es war,
was du vergossen, Herr.

Es glänzte.

Es warf uns dein Bild in die Augen, Herr.
Augen und Mund stehn so offen und leer, Herr.
Wir haben getrunken, Herr.
Das Blut und das Bild, das im Blut war, Herr.

Bete, Herr.
Wir sind nah.

TENEBRAE

We are near, Lord,
near and at hand.

Handled already, Lord,
clawed and clawing as though
the body of each of us were
your body, Lord.

Pray, Lord,
pray to us,
we are near.

Askew we went there,
went there to bend
down to the trough, to the crater.

To be watered we went there, Lord.

It was blood, it was
what you shed, Lord.

It gleamed.

It cast your image into our eyes, Lord.
Our eyes and our mouths are so open and empty, Lord.
We have drunk, Lord.
The blood and the image that was in the blood, Lord.

Pray, Lord.
We are near.

BLUME

Der Stein.
Der Stein in der Luft, dem ich folgte.
Dein Aug, so blind wie der Stein.

Wie waren
Hände,
wir schöpften die Finsternis leer, wir fanden
das Wort, das den Sommer heraufkam:
Blume.

Blume – ein Blindenwort.
Dein Aug und mein Aug:
sie sorgen
für Wasser.

Wachstum.
Herzwand um Herzwand
blättert hinzu.

Ein Wort noch, wie dies, und die Hämmer
schwingen im Freien.

FLOWER

The stone.
The stone in the air, which I followed.
Your eye, as blind as the stone.

We were
hands,
we baled the darkness empty, we found
the word that ascended summer:
flower.

Flower – a blind man's word.
Your eye and mine:
they see
to water.

Growth.
Heart wall upon heart wall
adds petals to it.

One more word like this, and the hammers
will swing over open ground.

WEISS UND LEICHT

Sicheldünen, ungezählt.

Im Windschatten, tausendfach: du.
Du und der Arm,
mit dem ich nackt zu dir hinwuchs,
Verlorne.

Die Strahlen. Sie wehn uns zuhauf.
Wir tragen den Schein, den Schmerz und den Namen.

Weiß,
was sich uns regt,
ohne Gewicht,
was wir tauschen.
Weiß und Leicht:
laß es wandern.

Die Fernen, mondnah, wie wir. Sie bauen.
Sie bauen die Klippe, wo
sich das Wandernde bricht,
sie bauen
weiter:
mit Lichtschaum und stäubender Welle.

Das Wandernde, klippenher winkend.
Die Stirnen
winkt es heran,
die Stirnen, die man uns lieh,
um der Spiegelung willen.

Die Stirnen.
Wir rollen mit ihnen dorthin.
Stirnengestade.

Schläfst du?

WHITE AND LIGHT

Sickle dunes, uncounted.

In wind-shadow, thousandfold, you.
You and the arm
with which naked I grew towards you,
lost one.

The beams. They blow us together.
We bear the brightness, the pain and the name.

White
what moves us,
without weight
what we exchange.
White and Light:
let it drift.

The distances, moon-near, like us. They build.
They build the cliff
where the drift breaks,
they build
on:
with light-froth and wave turned to foam.

The drift that beckons from cliffs.
It beckons
brows to come near,
those brows we were lent
for mirroring's sake.

The brows.
We roll with them there.
To a shore of brows.

Are you asleep?

Schlaf.

Meermühle geht,
eishell und ungehört,
in unsern Augen.

SPRACHGITTER

Augenrund zwischen den Stäben.

Flimmertier Lid
rudert nach oben,
gibt einen Blick frei.

Iris, Schwimmerin, traumlos und trüb:
der Himmel, herzgrau, muß nah sein.

Schräg, in der eisernen Tülle,
der blakende Span.
Am Lichtsinn
errätst du die Seele.

(Wär ich wie du. Wärst du wie ich.
Standen wir nicht
unter *einem* Passat?
Wir sind Fremde.)

Die Fliesen. Darauf,
dicht beieinander, die beiden
herzgrauen Lachen:
zwei
Mundvoll Schweigen.

Sleep.

Ocean mill turns,
ice-bright and unheard,
in our eyes.

LANGUAGE MESH

Eye's roundness between the bars.

Vibratile monad eyelid
propels itself upward,
releases a glance.

Iris, swimmer, dreamless and dreary:
the sky, heart-grey, must be near.

Athwart, in the iron holder,
the smoking splinter.
By its sense of light
you divine the soul.

(If I were like you. If you were like me.
Did we not stand
under *one* trade wind?
We are strangers.)

The flagstones. On them,
close to each other, the two
heart-grey puddles:
two
mouthsfull of silence.

SCHNEEBETT

Augen, weltblind, im Sterbegeklüft: Ich komm,
Hartwuchs im Herzen.
Ich komm.

Mondspiegel Steilwand. Hinab.
(Atemgeflecktes Geleucht. Strichweise Blut.
Wölkende Seele, noch einmal gestaltnah.
Zehnfingerschatten – verklammert.)

Augen weltblind,
Augen im Sterbegeklüft,
Augen Augen:

Das Schneebett unter uns beiden, das Schneebett.
Kristall um Kristall,
zeittief gegittert, wir fallen,
wir fallen und liegen und fallen.

Und fallen:
Wir waren. Wir sind.
Wir sind ein Fleisch mit der Nacht.
In den Gängen, den Gängen.

Eyes, world-blind, in the fissure of dying: I come,
callous growth in my heart.
I come.

Moon-mirror rock-face. Down.
(Shine spotted with breath. Blood in streaks.
Soul forming clouds, close to the true shape once more.
Ten-finger shadow, clamped.)

Eyes world-blind,
eyes in the fissure of dying,
eyes eyes:

The snow-bed under us both, the snow-bed.
Crystal on crystal,
meshed deep as time, we fall,
we fall and lie there and fall.

And fall:
We were. We are.
We are one flesh with the night.
In the passages, passages.

Kies und Geröll. Und ein Scherbenton, dünn,
als Zuspruch der Stunde.

Augentausch, endlich, zur Unzeit:
bildbeständig,
verholzt
die Netzhaut –:
das Ewigkeitszeichen.

Denkbar:
droben, im Weltgestänge,
sterngleich,
das Rot zweier Münder.

Hörbar (vor Morgen?): ein Stein,
der den andern zum Ziel nahm.

NIGHT

Pebbles and scree. And a shard note, thin,
as the hour's message of comfort.

Exchange of eyes, finite, at the wrong time:
image-constant,
lignified
the retina —:
the sign of eternity.

Conceivable:
up there, in the cosmic network of rails,
like stars,
the red of two mouths.

Audible (before dawn?): a stone
that made the other its target.

Ginsterlicht, gelb, die Hänge
eitern gen Himmel, der Dorn
wirbt um die Wunde, es läutet
darin, es ist Abend, das Nichts
rollt seine Meere zur Andacht,
das Blutsegel hält auf dich zu.

Trocken, verlandet
das Bett hinter dir, verschilft
seine Stunde, oben,
beim Stern, die milchigen
Priele schwatzen im Schlamm, Steindattel,
unten, gebuscht, klafft ins Gebläu, eine Staude
Vergänglichkeit, schön,
grüßt dein Gedächtnis.

(Kanntet ihr mich,
Hände? Ich ging
den gegabelten Weg, den ihr wiest, mein Mund
spie seinen Schotter, ich ging, meine Zeit,
wandernde Wächte, warf ihren Schatten – kanntet ihr mich?)

Hände, die dorn –
umworbene Wunde, es läutet,
Hände, das Nichts, seine Meere,
Hände, im Ginsterlicht, das
Blutsegel
hält auf dich zu.

Du
du lehrst
du lehrst deine Hände
du lehrst deine Hände du lehrst
du lehrst deine Hände
                        schlafen

MATIÈRE DE BRETAGNE

Gorselight, yellow, the slopes
suppurate heavenward, the thorn
woos the wound, bells ring
within, it is evening, Nothing
rolls its seas to the service,
the blood sail makes for you.

Dry, the bed behind you
fills with silt, its hour
clogs with rushes, above,
by the star, the milky
tideways jabber through mud, date shell,
below, bunched, yawns into blueness, a shrub
of transience, beautiful,
meets your memory, greets it.

(Did you know me,
hands? I went
the forked way you showed me, my mouth
spewed out its chippings, I went, my time,
a shifting snow-wall, cast its shadow – did you know me?)

Hands, the thorn-
wooed wound, hands,
Nothing is ringing its seas.
Hands, in the gorselight, the
blood sail
makes for you.

You
you teach
you teach your hands
you teach your hands you teach
you teach your hands
                    how to sleep

SCHUTTKAHN

Wasserstunde, der Schuttkahn
fährt uns zu Abend, wir haben,
wie er, keine Eile, ein totes
Warum steht am Heck.

. . . .

Geleichtert. Die Lunge, die Qualle
bläht sich zur Glocke, ein brauner
Seelenfortsatz erreicht
das hellgeatmete Nein.

RUBBLE BARGE

Water hour, the rubble barge
bears us to evening, like it
we're not in a hurry, a dead
Why stands at the stern.

. . . .

Lightened. The lung, the jellyfish
inflates itself to a bell, a brown
soul-prolongation arrives
at the No breathed bright.

ALLERSEELEN

Was hab ich
getan?
Die Nacht besamt, als könnt es
noch andere geben, nächtiger als
diese.

Vogelflug, Steinflug, tausend
beschriebene Bahnen. Blicke,
geraubt und gepflückt. Das Meer,
gekostet, vertrunken, verträumt. Eine Stunde,
seelenverfinstert. Die nächste, ein Herbstlicht,
dargebracht einem blinden
Gefühl, das des Wegs kam. Andere, viele,
ortlos und schwer aus sich selbst: erblickt und umgangen.
Findlinge, Sterne,
schwarz und voll Sprache: benannt
nach zerschwiegenem Schwur.

Und einmal (wann? auch dies ist vergessen):
den Widerhaken gefühlt,
wo der Puls den Gegentakt wagte.

ALL SOULS

What did I
do?
Seminated the night, as though
there could be others, more nocturnal than
this one.

Bird flight, stone flight, a thousand
described routes. Glances,
purloined and plucked. The sea,
tasted, drunk away, dreamed away. An hour
soul-eclipsed. The next, an autumn light,
offered up to a blind
feeling which came that way. Others, many,
with no place but their own heavy centres: glimpsed and avoided.
Foundlings, stars,
black, full of language: named
after an oath which silence annulled.

And once (when? that too is forgotten):
felt the barb
where my pulse dared the counter-beat.

ENTWURF EINER LANDSCHAFT

Rundgräber, unten. Im
Viertakt der Jahresschritt auf
den Steilstufen rings.

Laven, Basalte, weltherz-
durchglühtes Gestein.
Quelltuff,
wo uns das Licht wuchs, vor
dem Atem.

Ölgrün, meerdurchstäubt die
unbetretbare Stunde. Gegen
die Mitte zu, grau,
ein Steinsattel, drauf,
gebeult und verkohlt,
die Tierstirn mit
der strahligen Blesse.

DRAFT OF A LANDSCAPE

Circular graves, below. In
four-beat time the year's pace on
the steep steps around them.

Lavas, basalts, glowing
stone from the world's heart.
Wellspring tuff
where light grew for us, before
our breath.

Oilgreen, soaked with sea spray the
impassable hour. Toward
the centre, grey,
a stone saddle, and on it,
dented and charred,
the animal forehead with
its radiant blaze.

133

NIEDRIGWASSER. Wir sahen
die Seepocke, sahen
die Napfschnecke, sahen
die Nägel an unsern Händen.
Niemand schnitt uns das Wort von der Herzwand.

(Fahrten der Strandkrabbe, morgen,
Kriechfurchen, Wohngänge, Wind-
zeichnung im grauen
Schlick. Feinsand,
Grobsand, das
von den Wänden Gelöste, bei
andern Hartteilen, im
Schill.)

Ein Aug, heute,
gab es dem zweiten, beide,
geschlossen, folgten der Strömung zu
ihrem Schatten, setzten
die Fracht ab (*niemand
schnitt uns das Wort von der* – –), bauten
den Haken hinaus – eine Nehrung, vor
ein kleines
unbefahrbares Schweigen.

Low water. We saw
the balanid, saw
the limpet, saw
the nails on our hands.
No one cut the word for us from our heartwalls.

(Tracks of the shore crab, tomorrow,
crawl furrows, habitat trails, wind-
trace in the grey
silt, fine sand,
coarse sand, that
detached from the walls, with
other testaceous parts, in the
shell deposits.)

One eye, today,
gave it to a second, both,
closed, followed the current to
its shadow, unloaded
their cargo (*no one
cut the word for us from our* – –), shored outward
to the hook of land – a sand bar in front
of a small
unnavigable silence.

EIN AUGE, OFFEN

Stunden, maifarben, kühl.
Das nicht mehr zu Nennende, heiß,
hörbar im Mund.

Niemandes Stimme, wieder.

Schmerzende Augapfeltiefe:
das Lid
steht nicht im Wege, die Wimper
zählt nicht, was eintritt.

Die Träne, halb,
die schärfere Linse, beweglich,
holt dir die Bilder.

AN EYE, OPEN

Hours, May-coloured, cool.
The no more to be named, hot,
audible in the mouth.

No one's voice, again.

Aching depth of the eyeball:
the lid
does not stand in its way, the lash
does not count what goes in.

The tear, half,
the sharper lens, movable,
brings the images home to you.

OBEN, GERÄUSCHLOS, die
Fahrenden: Geier und Stern.

Unten, nach allem, wir,
zehn an der Zahl, das Sandvolk. Die Zeit,
wie denn auch nicht, sie hat
auch für uns eine Stunde, hier,
in der Sandstadt.

(Erzähl von den Brunnen, erzähl
von Brunnenkranz, Brunnenrad, von
Brunnenstuben – erzähl.

Zähl und erzähl, die Uhr,
auch diese, läuft ab.

Wasser: welch
ein Wort. Wir verstehen dich, Leben.)

Der Fremde, ungebeten, woher,
der Gast.
Sein triefendes Kleid.
Sein triefendes Auge.

(Erzähl uns von Brunnen, von –
Zähl und erzähl.
Wasser: welch
ein Wort.)

Sein Kleid-und-Auge, er steht,
wie wir, voller Nacht, er bekundet
Einsicht, er zählt jetzt,
wie wir, bis zehn
und nicht weiter.

Oben, die
Fahrenden
bleiben
unhörbar.

ABOVE, SOUNDLESS, the
travellers: vulture and star.

Below, after everything, we,
ten of us, sand people. Time,
how could it not, time has
an hour even for us, here,
in the sand city.

(Tell of the wells, tell
of the well-wreath, well-wheel, of
well-rooms – tell us.

Count and recount, the watch,
this one too, runs down.

Water: what
a word. We understand you, life.)

The stranger, uninvited, from where,
the guest.
His dripping clothes.
His dripping eye.

(Tell us of wells, of –
count and recount.
Water: what
a word.)

His clothes-and-eye, like us
he is filled with night, he betokens
insight, he counts now,
like us, up to ten
and no farther.

Above, the
travellers
remain
inaudible.

ENGFÜHRUNG

*

Verbracht ins
Gelände
mit der untrüglichen Spur:

Gras, auseinandergeschrieben. Die Steine, weiß,
mit den Schatten der Halme:
Lies nicht mehr – schau!
Schau nicht mehr – geh!

Geh, deine Stunde
hat keine Schwestern, du bist –
bist zuhause. Ein Rad, langsam,
rollt aus sich selber, die Speichen
klettern,
klettern auf schwärzlichem Feld, die Nacht
braucht keine Sterne, nirgends
fragt es nach dir.

*

Nirgends

fragt es nach dir –

Der Ort, wo sie lagen, er hat
einen Namen – er hat
keinen. Sie lagen nicht dort. Etwas
lag zwischen ihnen. Sie
sahn nicht hindurch.

THE STRAITENING

*

Driven into the
terrain
with the unmistakable track:

grass, written asunder. The stones, white,
with the shadows of grassblades:
Do not read any more – look!
Do not look any more – go!

Go, your hour
has no sisters, you are –
are at home. A wheel, slow,
rolls out of itself, the spokes
climb,
climb on a blackish field, the night
needs no stars, nowhere
does anyone ask after you.

*

          Nowhere

              does anyone ask after you –

The place where they lay, it has
a name – it has
none. They did not lie there. Something
lay between them. They
did not see through it.

Sahn nicht, nein,
redeten von
Worten. Keines
erwachte, der
Schlaf
kam über sie.

*

Kam, kam. Nirgends
fragt es –

Ich bins, ich,
ich lag zwischen euch, ich war
offen, war
hörbar, ich tickte euch zu, euer Atem
gehorchte, ich
bin es noch immer, ihr
schlaft ja.

*

Bin es noch immer –

Jahre.
Jahre, Jahre, ein Finger
tastet hinab und hinan, tastet
umher:
Nahtstellen, fühlbar, hier
klafft es weit auseinander, hier
wuchs es wieder zusammen – wer
deckte es zu?

*

Did not see, no,
spoke of
words. None
awoke,
sleep
came over them.

*

                           Came, came. Nowhere
                                     anyone asks –

It is I, I,
I lay between you, I was
open, was
audible, ticked at you, your breathing
obeyed, it is
I still, but then
you are asleep.

*

                                    It is I still –

years.
Years, years, a finger
feels down and up, feels
around:
seams, palpable, here
it is split wide open, here
it grew together again – who
covered it up?

*

Kam, kam.
Kam ein Wort, kam,
kam durch die Nacht,
wollt leuchten, wollt leuchten.

Asche.
Asche, Asche.
Nacht.
Nacht-und-Nacht. – Zum
Aug geh, zum feuchten.

*

                    Zum
                        Aug geh,
                            zum feuchten –

Orkane.
Orkane, von je,
Partikelgestöber, das andre,
du
weißts ja, wir
lasens im Buche, war
Meinung.

War, war
Meinung. Wie
faßten wir uns
an – an mit
diesen
Händen?

Came, came.
Came a word, came,
came through the night,
wanted to shine, wanted to shine.

Ash.
Ash, ash.
Night.
Night-and-night. – Go
to the eye, the moist one.

*

Go
to the eye,
the moist one –

Gales.
Gales, from the beginning of time,
whirl of particles, the other,
you
know it, though, we
read it in the book, was
opinion.

Was, was
opinion. How
did we touch
each other – each other with
these
hands?

Es stand auch geschrieben, daß.
Wo? Wir
taten ein Schweigen darüber,
giftgestillt, groß,
ein
grünes
Schweigen, ein Kelchblatt, es
hing ein Gedanke an Pflanzliches dran –

grün, ja,
hing, ja,
unter hämischem
Himmel.

An, ja,
Pflanzliches.

Ja.
Orkane, Par-
tikelgestöber, es blieb
Zeit, blieb,
es beim Stein zu versuchen – er
war gastlich, er
fiel nicht ins Wort. Wie
gut wir es hatten:

Körnig,
körnig und faserig. Stengelig,
dicht;
traubig und strahlig; nierig,
plattig und
klumpig; locker, ver-
ästelt –: er, es
fiel nicht ins Wort, es
sprach,
sprach gerne zu trockenen Augen, eh es sie schloß.

Sprach, sprach.
War, war.

There was written too, that.
Where? We
put a silence over it,
stilled with poison, great,
a
green
silence, a sepal, an
idea of vegetation attached to it –

green, yes,
attached, yes,
under a crafty
sky.

Of, yes,
vegetation.

Yes.
Gales, whirl of part-
icles, there was
time left, time
to try it out with the stone – it
was hospitable, it
did not cut in. How
lucky we were:

Grainy,
grainy and stringy. Stalky,
dense;
grapy and radiant; kidneyish,
flattish and
lumpy; loose, tang-
led –: he, it
did not cut in, it
spoke,
willingly spoke to dry eyes, before closing them.

Spoke, spoke.
Was, was.

Wir
ließen nicht locker, standen
inmitten, ein
Porenbau, und
es kam.

Kam auf uns zu, kam
hindurch, flickte
unsichtbar, flickte
an der letzten Membran,
und
die Welt, ein Tausendkristall,
schoß an, schoß an.

*

                    Schoß an, schoß an.
                             Dann –

Nächte, entmischt. Kreise,
grün oder blau, rote
Quadrate: die
Welt setzt ihr Innerstes ein
im Spiel mit den neuen
Stunden. – Kreise,

rot oder schwarz, helle
Quadrate, kein
Flugschatten,
kein
Meßtisch, keine
Rauchseele steigt und spielt mit.

We
would not let go, stood
in the midst, a
porous edifice, and
it came.

Came at us, came
through us, patched
invisibly, patched
away at the last membrane
and
the world, a millicrystal,
shot up, shot up.

*

Shot up, shot up.
Then –

Nights, demixed. Circles,
green or blue, scarlet
squares: the
world puts its inmost reserves
into the game with the new
hours. – Circles,

red or black, bright
squares, no
flight shadow,
no
measuring table, no
smoke soul ascends or joins in.

*

In der Eulenflucht, beim
versteinerten Aussatz,
bei
unsern geflohenen Händen, in
der jüngsten Verwerfung,
überm
Kugelfang an
der verschütteten Mauer:

sichtbar, aufs
neue: die
Rillen, die

Chöre, damals, die
Psalmen. Ho, ho-
sianna.

Also
stehen noch Tempel. Ein
Stern
hat wohl noch Licht.
Nichts,
nichts ist verloren.

Ho-
sianna.

In der Eulenflucht, hier,
die Gespräche, taggrau,
der Grundwasserspuren.

*

                                        Ascends or
                                                joins in –

At owl's flight, near
the petrified scabs,
near
our fled hands, in
the latest rejection,
above
the rifle-range near
the buried wall:

visible, once
more: the
grooves, the

choirs at that time, the
psalms. Ho, ho-
sanna.

So
there are temples yet. A
star
probably still has light.
Nothing,
nothing is lost.

Ho-
sanna.

At owl's flight, here,
the conversations, day-grey,
of the water-level traces.

*

(– – taggrau,
der
Grundwasserspuren –

Verbracht
ins Gelände
mit
der untrüglichen
Spur:

Gras.
Gras,
auseinandergeschrieben.)

*

         (– – day-grey,
                  of
                     the water-level traces –

Driven into the
terrain
with
the unmistakable
track:

Grass.
Grass,
written asunder.)

FROM
Die Niemandsrose
(1963)

Es war Erde in ihnen, und
sie gruben.

Sie gruben und gruben, so ging
ihr Tag dahin, ihre Nacht. Und sie lobten nicht Gott,
der, so hörten sie, alles dies wollte,
der, so hörten sie, alles dies wußte.

Sie gruben und hörten nichts mehr;
sie wurden nicht weise, erfanden kein Lied,
erdachten sich keinerlei Sprache.
Sie gruben.

Es kam eine Stille, es kam auch ein Sturm,
es kamen die Meere alle.
Ich grabe, du gräbst, und es gräbt auch der Wurm,
und das Singende dort sagt: Sie graben.

O einer, o keiner, o niemand, o du:
Wohin gings, da's nirgendhin ging?
O du gräbst und ich grab, und ich grab mich dir zu,
und am Finger erwacht uns der Ring.

THERE WAS EARTH INSIDE THEM, and
they dug.

They dug and they dug, so their day
went by for them, their night. And they did not praise God,
who, so they heard, wanted all this,
who, so they heard, knew all this.

They dug and heard nothing more;
they did not grow wise, invented no song,
thought up for themselves no language.
They dug.

There came a stillness, and there came a storm,
and all the oceans came.
I dig, you dig, and the worm digs too,
and that singing out there says: They dig.

O one, o none, o no one, o you:
Where did the way lead when it led nowhere?
O you dig and I dig, and I dig towards you,
and on our finger the ring awakes.

Bei Wein und Verlorenheit, bei
beider Neige:

ich ritt durch den Schnee, hörst du,
ich ritt Gott in die Ferne – die Nähe, er sang,
es war
unser letzter Ritt über
die Menschen-Hürden.

Sie duckten sich, wenn
sie uns über sich hörten, sie
schrieben, sie
logen unser Gewieher
um in eine
ihrer bebilderten Sprachen.

OVER WINE AND LOSTNESS, over
the running-out of both:

I rode through the snow, do you hear,
I rode God into farness – nearness, he sang,
it was
our last ride over
the human hurdles.

They ducked when
they heard us above their heads, they
wrote, they
lied our whinnying
into one
of their be-imaged languages.

ZÜRICH, ZUM STORCHEN

Für Nelly Sachs

Vom Zuviel war die Rede, vom
Zuwenig. Von Du
und Aber-Du, von
der Trübung durch Helles, von
Jüdischem, von
deinem Gott.

Da-
von.
Am Tag einer Himmelfahrt, das
Münster stand drüben, es kam
mit einigem Gold übers Wasser.

Von deinem Gott war die Rede, ich sprach
gegen ihn, ich
ließ das Herz, das ich hatte,
hoffen:
auf
sein höchstes, umröcheltes, sein
haderndes Wort –

Dein Aug sah mir zu, sah hinweg,
dein Mund
sprach sich dem Aug zu, ich hörte:

Wir
wissen ja nicht, weißt du,
wir
wissen ja nicht,
was
gilt.

ZÜRICH, THE STORK INN

For Nelly Sachs

Of too much was our talk, of
too little. Of the You
and You-Again, of
how clarity troubles, of
Jewishness, of
your God.

Of
that.
On the day of an ascension, the
Minster stood over there, it sent
some gold across the water.

Of your God was our talk, I spoke
against him, I
let the heart that I had
hope:
for
his highest, death-rattled, his
quarrelling word –

Your eye looked on, looked away,
your mouth
spoke its way to the eye, and I heard:

We
don't know, you know,
we
don't know, do we?,
what
counts.

SOVIEL GESTIRNE, die
man uns hinhält. Ich war,
als ich dich ansah – wann? –,
draußen bei
den andern Welten.

O diese Wege, galaktisch,
o diese Stunde, die uns
die Nächte herüberwog in
die Last unsrer Namen. Es ist,
ich weiß es, nicht wahr,
daß wir lebten, es ging
blind nur ein Atem zwischen
Dort und Nicht-da und Zuweilen,
kometenhaft schwirrte ein Aug
auf Erloschenes zu, in den Schluchten,
da, wo's verglühte, stand
zitzenprächtig die Zeit,
an der schon empor- und hinab-
und hinwegwuchs, was
ist oder war oder sein wird –,

ich weiß,
ich weiß und du weißt, wir wußten,
wir wußten nicht, wir
waren ja da und nicht dort,
und zuweilen, wenn
nur das Nichts zwischen uns stand, fanden
wir ganz zueinander.

SO MANY CONSTELLATIONS that
are held out to us. I was,
when I looked at you – when? –
outside by
the other worlds.

O these ways, galactic,
O this hour, that weighed
nights over for us into
the burden of our names. It is,
I know, not true
that we lived, there moved,
blindly, no more than a breath between
there and not-there, and at times
our eyes whirred comet-like
toward things extinguished, in chasms,
and where they had burnt out,
splendid with teats, stood Time
on which already grew up
and down and away all that
is or was or will be – ,

I know,
I know and you know, we knew,
we did not know, we
were there, after all, and not there
and at times when
only the void stood between us we got
all the way to each other.

DEIN
HINÜBERSEIN heute Nacht.
Mit Worten holt ich dich wieder, da bist du,
alles ist wahr und ein Warten
auf Wahres.

Es klettert die Bohne vor
unserm Fenster: denk
wer neben uns aufwächst und
ihr zusieht.

Gott, das lasen wir, ist
ein Teil und ein zweiter, zerstreuter:
im Tod
all der Gemähten
wächst er sich zu.

Dorthin
führt uns der Blick,
mit dieser
Hälfte
haben wir Umgang.

Your
BEING BEYOND in the night.
With words I fetched you back, there you are,
all is true and a waiting
for truth.

In front of our window
the bean-plant climbs: think
who is growing beside us and
watches it.

God, so we read, is
a part and a second, a scattered one:
in the death
of all those mown down
he grows himself whole.

There
our looking leads us,
with this
half
we keep up relations.

ZU BEIDEN HÄNDEN, da
wo die Sterne mir wuchsen, fern
allen Himmeln, nah
allen Himmeln:
Wie
wacht es sich da! Wie
tut sich die Welt uns auf, mitten
durch uns!

Du bist,
wo dein Aug ist, du bist
oben, bist
unten, ich
finde hinaus.

O diese wandernde leere
gastliche Mitte. Getrennt,
fall ich dir zu, fällst
du mir zu, einander
entfallen, sehn wir
hindurch:

Das
Selbe
hat uns
verloren, das
Selbe
hat uns
vergessen, das
Selbe
hat uns — —

On either hand, there
where stars grew for me, far
from all heavens, near
all heavens:
How
one's awake there! How
the world opens for us, right through the midst
of ourselves!

You are
where your eye is, you are
above, are
below, I
find my way out.

O this wandering empty
hospitable midst. Apart,
I fall to you, you
fall to me, fallen away
from each other, we see
through:

One
and the same
has
lost us, one
and the same
has
forgotten us, one
and the same
has ——

ZWÖLF JAHRE

Die wahr-
gebliebene, wahr-
gewordene Zeile: ... *dein
Haus in Paris – zur
Opferstatt deiner Hände*.

Dreimal durchatmet,
dreimal durchglänzt.

. . . .

Es wird stumm, es wird taub
hinter den Augen.
Ich sehe das Gift blühn.
In jederlei Wort und Gestalt.

Geh. Komm.
Die Liebe löscht ihren Namen: sie
schreibt sich dir zu.

TWELVE YEARS

The line
that remained, that
became true: ... *your*
house in Paris — become
the altarpiece of your hands.

Breathed through thrice,
shone through thrice.

. . . .

It's turning dumb, turning deaf
behind our eyes.
I see the poison flower.
In all manner of words and shapes.

Go. Come.
Love blots out its name: to
you it ascribes itself.

MIT ALLEN GEDANKEN ging ich
hinaus aus der Welt: da warst du,
du meine Leise, du meine Offne, und –
du empfingst uns.

Wer
sagt, daß uns alles erstarb,
da uns das Aug brach?
Alles erwachte, alles hob an.

Groß kam eine Sonne geschwommen, hell
standen ihr Seele und Seele entgegen, klar,
gebieterisch schwiegen sie ihr
ihre Bahn vor.

Leicht
tat sich dein Schoß auf, still
stieg ein Hauch in den Äther,
und was sich wölkte, wars nicht,
wars nicht Gestalt und von uns her,
wars nicht
so gut wie ein Name?

WITH ALL MY THOUGHTS I
went out of the world: and there you were,
you my quiet, my open one, and –
you received us.

Who
says that everything died for us
when our eyes broke?
Everything awakened, everything began.

Great, a sun came drifting, bright
a soul and a soul confronted it, clear,
masterfully their silence mapped out
an orbit for the sun.

Easily
your lap opened, tranquilly
a breath rose up to the aether
and that which made clouds, was it not,
was it not a shape come from us,
was it not
as good as a name?

DIE SCHLEUSE

Über aller dieser deiner
Trauer: kein
zweiter Himmel.

. . . .

An einen Mund,
dem es ein Tausendwort war,
verlor –
verlor ich ein Wort,
das mir verblieben war:
Schwester.

An
die Vielgötterei
verlor ich ein Wort, das mich suchte:
Kaddisch.

Durch
die Schleuse mußt ich,
das Wort in die Salzflut zurück-
und hinaus- und hinüberzuretten:
Jiskor.

THE LOCK GATE

Above all this mourning
of yours: no
second heaven.

....

To a mouth
for which it was one of a thousand
I lost –
I lost a word
that had remained with me:
sister.

To
the worship of many gods
I lost a word that was looking for me:
Kaddish.

Through
the lock gate I had to go
to save the word back
to the salt waters and
out and across:
Yiskor.

STUMME HERBSTGERÜCHE. Die
Sternblume, ungeknickt, ging
zwischen Heimat und Abgrund durch
dein Gedächtnis.

Eine fremde Verlorenheit war
gestalthaft zugegen, du hättest
beinah
gelebt.

DUMB AUTUMN SMELLS. The
marguerite, unbroken, passed
between home and chasm through
your memory.

A strange lostness was
palpably present, almost
you would
have lived.

EIS, EDEN

Es ist ein Land Verloren,
da wächst ein Mond im Ried,
und das mit uns erfroren,
es glüht umher und sieht.

Es sieht, denn es hat Augen,
die helle Erden sind.
Die Nacht, die Nacht, die Laugen.
Es sieht, das Augenkind.

Es sieht, es sieht, wir sehen,
ich sehe dich, du siehst.
Das Eis wird auferstehen,
eh sich die Stunde schließt.

ICE, EDEN

There is a country Lost,
a moon grows in its reeds,
where all that died of frost
as we did, glows and sees.

It sees, for it has eyes,
each eye an earth, and bright.
The night, the night, the lyes.
This eye-child's gift is sight.

It sees, it sees, we see,
I see you, you see me.
Before this hour has ended
ice will rise from the dead.

PSALM

Niemand knetet uns wieder aus Erde und Lehm,
niemand bespricht unsern Staub.
Niemand.

Gelobt seist du, Niemand.
Dir zulieb wollen
wir blühn.
Dir
entgegen.

Ein Nichts
waren wir, sind wir, werden
wir bleiben, blühend:
die Nichts-, die
Niemandsrose.

Mit
dem Griffel seelenhell,
dem Staubfaden himmelswüst,
der Krone rot
vom Purpurwort, das wir sangen
über, o über
dem Dorn.

PSALM

No one moulds us again out of earth and clay,
no one conjures our dust.
No one.

Praised be your name, no one.
For your sake
we shall flower.
Towards
you.

A nothing
we were, are, shall
remain, flowering:
the nothing-, the
no one's rose.

With
our pistil soul-bright,
with our stamen heaven-ravaged,
our corolla red
with the crimson word which we sang
over, O over
the thorn.

TÜBINGEN, JÄNNER

Zur Blindheit über-
redete Augen.
Ihre – »ein
Rätsel ist Rein-
entsprungenes« –, ihre
Erinnerung an
schwimmende Hölderlintürme, möwen-
umschwirrt.

Besuche ertrunkener Schreiner bei
diesen
tauchenden Worten:

Käme,
käme ein Mensch,
käme ein Mensch zur Welt, heute, mit
dem Lichtbart der
Patriarchen: er dürfte,
spräch er von dieser
Zeit, er
dürfte
nur lallen und lallen,
immer-, immer-
zuzu.

(»Pallaksch. Pallaksch.«)

Eyes talked into
blindness.
Their – "an enigma is
the purely
originated" –, their
memory of
Hölderlin towers afloat, circled
by whirring gulls.

Visits of drowned joiners to
these
submerging words:

Should,
should a man,
should a man come into the world, today, with
the shining beard of the
patriarchs: he could,
if he spoke of this
time, he
could
only babble and babble
over, over
againagain.

("Pallaksh. Pallaksh.")

CHYMISCH

Schweigen, wie Gold gekocht, in
verkohlten
Händen.

Große, graue,
wie alles Verlorene nahe
Schwestergestalt:

Alle die Namen, alle die mit-
verbrannten
Namen. Soviel
zu segnende Asche. Soviel
gewonnenes Land
über
den leichten, so leichten
Seelen-
ringen.

Große. Graue. Schlacken-
lose.

Du, damals.
Du mit der fahlen,
aufgebissenen Knospe.
Du in der Weinflut.

(Nicht wahr, auch uns
entließ diese Uhr?
Gut,
gut, wie dein Wort hier vorbeistarb.)

Schweigen, wie Gold gekocht, in
verkohlten, verkohlten

ALCHEMICAL

Silence, cooked like gold, in
charred
hands.

Great, grey
sisterly shape
near like all that is lost:

All the names, all those
names
burnt with the rest. So much
ash to be blessed. So much
land won
above
the weightless, so weightless
rings
of souls.

Great, grey one. Cinder-
less.

You, then.
You with the pale
bit-open bud,
you in the wine-flood.

(Us too, don't you think,
this clock dismissed?
Good,
good, how your word died past us here.)

Silence, cooked like gold, in
charred, charred

Händen.
Finger, rauchdünn. Wie Kronen, Luftkronen
um – –

Große. Graue. Fährte-
lose.
König-
liche.

hands.
Fingers, insubstantial as smoke. Like crests, crests of air
around – –

Great, grey one. Wake-
less.
Re-
gal one.

...RAUSCHT DER BRUNNEN

Ihr gebet-, ihr lästerungs-, ihr
gebetscharfen Messer
meines
Schweigens.

Ihr meine mit mir ver-
krüppelnden Worte, ihr
meine geraden.

Und du:
du, du, du
mein täglich wahr- und wahrer-
geschundenes Später
der Rosen –:

Wieviel, o wieviel
Welt. Wieviel
Wege.

Krücke du, Schwinge. Wir – –

Wir werden das Kinderlied singen, das,
hörst du, das
mit den Men, mit den Schen, mit den Menschen, ja das
mit dem Gestrüpp und mit
dem Augenpaar, das dort bereitlag als
Träne-und-
Träne.

...PLASHES THE FOUNTAIN

You prayer-, you blasphemy-, you
prayer-sharp knives
of my
silence.

You my words being crippled
together with me, you
my hale ones.

And you:
you, you, you
my later of roses
daily worn true and
more true –:

How much, O how much
world. How many
paths.

You crutch, you wing. We – –

We shall sing the nursery rhyme, that one,
do you hear, that one
with the hu, with the man, with the human being, the one
with the scrub and with
the pair of eyes that lay ready there as
tear-upon-
tear.

Es ist nicht mehr
diese
zuweilen mit dir
in die Stunde gesenkte
Schwere. Es ist
eine andre.

Es ist das Gewicht, das die Leere zurückhält,
die mit-
ginge mit dir.
Es hat, wie du, keinen Namen. Vielleicht
seid ihr dasselbe. Vielleicht
nennst auch du mich einst
so.

IT IS NO LONGER
this
heaviness
lowered at times together with you
into the hour. It is
another.

It is the weight holding back the void
that would
accompany you.
Like you, it has no name. Perhaps
you two are one and the same. Perhaps
one day you also will call
me so.

RADIX, MATRIX

Wie man zum Stein spricht, wie
du,
mir vom Abgrund her, von
einer Heimat her Ver-
schwisterte, Zu-
geschleuderte, du,
du mir vorzeiten,
du mir im Nichts einer Nacht,
du in der Aber-Nacht Be-
gegnete, du
Aber-Du –:

Damals, da ich nicht da war,
damals, da du
den Acker abschrittst, allein:

Wer,
wer wars, jenes
Geschlecht, jenes gemordete, jenes
schwarz in den Himmel stehende:
Rute und Hode –?

(Wurzel.
Wurzel Abrahams. Wurzel Jesse. Niemandes
Wurzel – o
unser.)

Ja,
wie man zum Stein spricht, wie
du
mit meinen Händen dorthin
und ins Nichts greifst, so
ist, was hier ist:

auch dieser
Fruchtboden klafft,

RADIX, MATRIX

As one speaks to stone, like
you,
from the chasm, from
a home become a
sister to me, hurled
towards me, you,
you that long ago,
you in the nothingness of a night,
you in the multi-night en-
countered, you
multi-you –:

At that time, when I was not there,
at that time when you
paced the ploughed field, alone:

Who,
who was it, that
lineage, the murdered, that looms
black into the sky:
rod and bulb –?

(Root.
Abraham's root. Jesse's root. No one's
root – O
ours.)

Yes,
as one speaks to stone, as
you
with my hands grope into there,
and into nothing, such
is what is here:

this fertile
soil too gapes,

dieses
Hinab
ist die eine der wild-
blühenden Kronen.

MANDORLA

In der Mandel – was steht in der Mandel?
Das Nichts.
Es steht das Nichts in der Mandel.
Da steht es und steht.

Im Nichts – wer steht da? Der König.
Da steht der König, der König.
Da steht er und steht.

    Judenlocke, wirst nicht grau.

Und dein Aug – wohin steht dein Auge?
Dein Aug steht der Mandel entgegen.
Dein Aug, dem Nichts stehts entgegen.
Es steht zum König.
So steht es und steht.

    Menschenlocke, wirst nicht grau.
    Leere Mandel, königsblau.

this
going down
is one of the
crests growing wild.

MANDORLA

In the almond – what dwells in the almond?
Nothing.
What dwells in the almond is Nothing.
There it dwells and dwells.

In Nothing – what dwells there? The King.
There the King dwells, the King.
There he dwells and dwells.

      Jew's curl, you'll not turn grey.

And your eye – on what does your eye dwell?
On the almond your eye dwells.
Your eye, on Nothing it dwells.
Dwells on the King, to him remains loyal, true.
So it dwells and dwells.

      Human curl, you'll not turn grey.
      Empty almond, royal-blue.

AN NIEMAND GESCHMIEGT mit der Wange –
an dich, Leben.
An dich, mit dem Handstumpf
gefundnes.

Ihr Finger.
Fern, unterwegs,
an den Kreuzungen, manchmal,
die Rast
bei freigelassenen Gliedern,
auf
dem Staubkissen Einst.

Verholzter Herzvorrat: der
schwelende
Liebes- und Lichtknecht.

Ein Flämmchen halber
Lüge noch in
dieser, in jener
übernächtigen Pore,
die ihr berührt.

Schlüsselgeräusche oben,
im Atem-
Baum über euch:
das letzte
Wort, das euch ansah,
soll jetzt bei sich sein und bleiben.

. . . .

An dich geschmiegt, mit
dem Handstumpf gefundenes
Leben.

CHEEK NESTLED UP against no one –
against you, life.
Against you, found
with the stump of a hand.

You fingers.
Far off, on your way,
at the crossroads, at times,
rest
with limbs relaxed,
on
the pillow of dust called Once.

Heartstore lignified: the
smouldering
slave to love and light.

A flicker of half-
lies left in
this, in that
insomnia-weary pore
that you touch.

Key noises above,
in the breath-
tree above you:
the last
word to see you
shall be at home now, and stay.

. . . .

Nestled up against you,
life,
found with the stump of a hand.

ZWEIHÄUSIG, EWIGER, bist du, un-
bewohnbar. Darum
baun wir und bauen. Darum
steht sie, diese
erbärmliche Bettstatt, – im Regen,
da steht sie.

Komm, Geliebte.
Daß wir hier liegen, das
ist die Zwischenwand –: Er
hat dann genug an sich selber, zweimal.

Laß ihn, er
habe sich ganz, als das Halbe
und abermals Halbe. Wir,
wir sind das Regenbett, er
komme und lege uns trocken.

. . . .

Er kommt nicht, et legt uns nicht trocken.

À LA POINTE ACÉRÉE

Es liegen die Erze bloß, die Kristalle,
die Drusen.
Ungeschriebenes, zu
Sprache verhärtet, legt
einen Himmel frei.

(Nach oben verworfen, zutage,
überquer, so
liegen auch wir.

TWO-HOUSED, ETERNAL ONE, you are, un-
inhabitable. That is why
we build and build. That is why
it stands, this
pitiable bedstead, – in the rain,
there it stands.

Come, beloved.
That we may lie here, this
is the partition –: He
will then suffice himself, twice over.

Leave him, let
him have himself wholly, as the half
and half again. We,
we are the rain-bed, let him
come and lay us down dry.

....

He does not come, does not lay us down dry.

À LA POINTE ACÉRÉE

The ores are laid bare, the crystals,
the geodes.
Unwritten things, hardened
into language, lay bare
a sky.

(Thrown out upward, revealed,
crossways, so
we too are lying.

Tür du davor einst, Tafel
mit dem getöteten
Kreidestern drauf:
ihn
hat nun ein – lesendes? – Aug.)

Wege dorthin.
Waldstunde an
der blubbernden Radspur entlang.
Auf-
gelesene
kleine, klaffende
Buchecker: schwärzliches
Offen, von
Fingergedanken befragt
nach – –
wonach?

Nach
dem Unwiederholbaren, nach
ihm, nach
allem.

Blubbernde Wege dorthin.

Etwas, das gehn kann, grußlos
wie Herzgewordenes,
kommt.

Door in front of it once, tablet
with the killed
chalk star on it: that
a – reading? – eye has now.)

Ways to that place.
Forest hour alongside
the spluttering wheeltrack.
Col-
lected
small, gaping
beechnuts: blackish
openness, questioned
by finger thoughts
about – –
about what?

About
the unrepeatable, about
it, about
everything.

Spluttering tracks to that place.

Something mobile, ungreeting
as all that's turned into heart,
is coming.

DIE HELLEN
STEINE gehn durch die Luft, die hell-
weißen, die Licht-
bringer.

Sie wollen
nicht niedergehen, nicht stürzen,
nicht treffen. Sie gehen
auf,
wie die geringen
Heckenrosen, so tun sie sich auf,
sie schweben
dir zu, du meine Leise,
du meine Wahre –:

ich seh dich, du pflückst sie mit meinen
neuen, meinen
Jedermannshänden, du tust sie
ins Abermals-Helle, das niemand
zu weinen braucht noch zu nennen.

THE BRIGHT
STONES pass through the air, the brightly
white, the light-
bringers.

They will
not go down, will not drop,
will not hit. They open
up
like the flimsy
hedge briars, like them they unfurl,
they hover
toward you, my quiet one,
my true one —:

I see you, you pick them with
my new, my
everyman's hands, you put them
into the Bright-Once-More which no one
needs to weep or to name.

ANABASIS

Dieses
schmal zwischen Mauern geschriebne
unwegsam-wahre
Hinauf und Zurück
in die herzhelle Zukunft.

Dort.

Silben-
mole, meer-
farben, weit
ins Unbefahrne hinaus.

Dann:
Bojen-,
Kummerbojen-Spalier
mit den
sekundenschön hüpfenden
Atemreflexen –: Leucht-
glockentöne (dum-,
dun-, un-,
unde suspirat
cor),
aus-
gelöst, ein-
gelöst, unser.

Sichtbares, Hörbares, das
frei-
werdende Zeltwort:

Mitsammen.

ANABASIS

This
narrow sign between walls
the impassable-true
Upward and Back
to the heart-bright future.

There.

Syllable-
mole, sea-
coloured, far out
into the unnavigated.

Then:
buoys,
espalier of sorrow-buoys
with those
breath reflexes leaping and
lovely for seconds only –: light-
bellsounds (dum-,
dun-, un-,
*unde suspirat
cor*),
re-
leased, re-
deemed, ours.

Visible, audible thing, the
tent-
word growing free:

Together.

NACHMITTAG MIT ZIRKUS UND ZITADELLE

In Brest, vor den Flammenringen,
im Zelt, wo der Tiger sprang,
da hört ich dich, Endlichkeit, singen,
da sah ich dich, Mandelstamm.

Der Himmel hing über der Reede,
die Möwe hing über dem Kran.
Das Endliche sang, das Stete, –
du, Kanonenboot, heißt »Baobab«.

Ich grüßte die Trikolore
mit einem russischen Wort –
Verloren war Unverloren,
das Herz ein befestigter Ort.

AFTERNOON WITH CIRCUS
AND CITADEL

In Brest, before hoops of flame,
in the tent where the tiger leapt,
there, Finite, I heard you sing,
there I saw you, Mandelstam.

The sky hung above the roadstead,
the gull hung above the crane.
What is finite sang, what is constant –
you, gunboat, are called "Baobab".

I saluted the tricolore
speaking a Russian word –
things lost were things not lost,
the heart was a place made fast.

BEI TAG

Hasenfell-Himmel. Noch immer
schreibt eine deutliche Schwinge.

Auch ich, erinnere dich,
Staub-
farbene, kam
als ein Kranich.

KERMORVAN

Du Tausendgüldenkraut-Sternchen,
du Erle, du Buche, du Farn:
mit euch Nahen geh ich ins Ferne, –
Wir gehen dir, Heimat, ins Garn.

Schwarz hängt die Kirschlorbeertraube
beim bärtigen Palmenschaft.
Ich liebe, ich hoffe, ich glaube, –
die kleine Steindattel klafft.

Ein Spruch spricht – zu wem? Zu sich selber:
Servir Dieu est régner, – ich kann
ihn lesen, ich kann, es wird heller,
fort aus Kannitverstan.

IN THE DAYTIME

Hare's pelt sky. Even now
a clear wing writes.

I too, remember,
dust-
coloured one, arrived
as a crane.

KERMORVAN

You tiny centaury star,
you alder, beech and fern:
with you near ones I make for afar, –
to our homeland, snared, we return.

By the bearded palm tree's trunk
black hangs the laurel-seed grape.
I love, I hope, I have faith, –
the little date shell's agape.

A word speaks – to whom? To itself:
Servir Dieu est régner, – I can
read it, I can, it grows brighter,
away from "kannitverstan".

ICH HABE BAMBUS GESCHNITTEN:
für dich, mein Sohn.
Ich habe gelebt.

Diese morgen fort-
getragene Hütte, sie
steht.

Ich habe nicht mitgebaut: du
weißt nicht, in was für
Gefäße ich den
Sand um mich her tat, vor Jahren, auf
Geheiß und Gebot. Der deine
kommt aus dem Freien – er bleibt
frei.

Das Rohr, das hier Fuß faßt, morgen
steht es noch immer, wohin dich
die Seele auch hinspielt im Un-
gebundnen.

WAS GESCHAH? Der Stein trat aus dem Berge.
Wer erwachte? Du und ich.
Sprache, Sprache. Mit-Stern. Neben-Erde.
Ärmer. Offen. Heimatlich.

Wohin gings? Gen Unverklungen.
Mit dem Stein gings, mit uns zwein.
Herz und Herz. Zu schwer befunden.
Schwerer werden. Leichter sein.

I HAVE CUT BAMBOO:
for you, my son.
I have lived.

This hut to
be dismantled tomorrow, it
stands.

I did not join in the building: you
don't know in what kind
of vessels I put
the sand from around me, years ago, thus
commanded and bidden. Yours
comes from the open places – it stays
open.

The reed that takes root here, tomorrow
still it will stand, wherever
in the unbound your soul may
play you.

WHAT OCCURRED? The boulder left the mountain.
Who awakened? You and I.
Language, language. Co-earth. Fellow-planet.
Poorer. Open. Homelandly.

The course? Towards the unsubsided.
Your course and mine was the boulder's flight.
Heart and heart. Adjudged too heavy.
Grow more heavy. Be more light.

IN EINS

Dreizehnter Feber. Im Herzmund
erwachtes Schibboleth. Mit dir,
Peuple
de Paris. *No pasarán*.

Schäfchen zur Linken: er, Abadias,
der Greis aus Huesca, kam mit den Hunden
über das Feld, im Exil
stand weiß eine Wolke
menschlichen Adels, er sprach
uns das Wort in die Hand, das wir brauchten, es war
Hirten-Spanisch, darin,

im Eislicht des Kreuzers »Aurora«:
die Bruderhand, winkend mit der
von den wortgroßen Augen
genommenen Binde – Petropolis, der
Unvergessenen Wanderstadt lag
auch dir toskanisch zu Herzen.

Friede den Hütten!

IN ONE

Thirteenth of February. Shibboleth
roused in the heart's mouth. With you,
peuple
de Paris. *No pasarán.*

Little sheep to the left: he, Abadias,
the old man from Huesca, came with his dogs
over the field, in exile
white hung a cloud
of human nobility, into our hands
he spoke the word that we needed, it was
shepherd-Spanish, and in it

in icelight of the cruiser "Aurora":
the brotherly hand, waving with
the blindfold removed from
his word-wide eyes – Petropolis, the
roving city of those unforgotten,
was Tuscanly close to your heart also.

Peace to the cottages!

HINAUSGEKRÖNT,
hinausgespien in die Nacht.

Bei welchen
Sternen! Lauter
graugeschlagenes Herzhammersilber. Und
Berenikes Haupthaar, auch hier, – ich flocht,
ich zerflocht,
ich flechte, zerflechte.
Ich flechte.

Blauschlucht, in dich
treib ich das Gold. Auch mit ihm, dem
bei Huren und Dirnen vertanen,
komm ich und komm ich. Zu dir,
Geliebte.

Auch mit Fluch und Gebet. Auch mit jeder
der über mich hin-
schwirrenden Keulen: auch sie in eins
geschmolzen, auch sie
phallisch gebündelt zu dir,
Garbe-und-Wort.

Mit Namen, getränkt
von jedem Exil.
Mit Namen und Samen,
mit Namen, getaucht
in alle
Kelche, die vollstehn mit deinem
Königsblut, Mensch, – in alle
Kelche der großen
Ghetto-Rose, aus der
du uns ansiehst, unsterblich von soviel
auf Morgenwegen gestorbenen Toden.

(Und wir sangen die Warschowjanka.
Mit verschilften Lippen, Petrarca.
In Tundra-Ohren, Petrarca.)

CROWNED OUT,
spewed out into night.

Under what
stars! So much
grey-beaten heart-hammer silver. And
Berenice's head of hair, here too. – I plaited,
I unplaited,
I plait, unplait.
I plait.

Blue chasm, into you
I drive the gold. Bringing that too
wasted on whores and harlots,
I go and go. To you,
beloved.

And with curses and prayer. And with each
of the cudgels whirring
over me: they too fused
into one, they too
phallically bunched towards you,
both sheaf and word.

With names, watered
by every exile.
With names and seeds,
with names dipped
into all
the calyxes that are full of your
regal blood, man, – into all
the calyxes of the great
ghetto-rose, from which
you look at us, immortal with so many
deaths died on morning errands.

(And we sang the Warshawyanka
with lips grown reedy, Petrarca.
Into tundra-ears, Petrarca.)

Und es steigt eine Erde herauf, die unsre,
diese.
Und wir schicken
keinen der Unsern hinunter
zu dir,
Babel.

LES GLOBES

In den verfahrenen Augen – lies da:

die Sonnen-, die Herzbahnen, das
sausend-schöne Umsonst.
Die Tode und alles
aus ihnen Geborene. Die
Geschlechterkette,
die hier bestattet liegt und
die hier noch hängt, im Äther,
Abgründe säumend. Aller
Gesichter Schrift, in die sich
schwirrender Wortsand gebohrt – Kleinewiges,
Silben.

Alles,
das Schwerste noch, war
flügge, nichts
hielt zurück.

And an earth rises up, ours,
this one.
And we'll send
none of our people down
to you,
Babel.

LES GLOBES

In the eyes all awry – read there:

the sun, the heart orbits, the
whizzing, lovely In Vain.
The deaths and all that
to which they gave birth. The
chain of generations
that lies buried here and
hangs here still, in the aether,
and borders abysses. All the script
on those faces into which
whirring word-sand drilled itself – tiny eternities,
syllables.

All things,
even the heaviest, were
fledged, nothing
held back.

HÜTTENFENSTER

Das Aug, dunkel:
als Hüttenfenster. Es sammelt,
was Welt war, Welt bleibt: den Wander-
Osten, die
Schwebenden, die
Menschen-und-Juden,
das Volk-vom-Gewölk, magnetisch
ziehts, mit Herzfingern, an
dir, Erde:
du kommst, du kommst,
wohnen werden wir, wohnen, etwas

– ein Atem? ein Name? –

geht im Verwaisten umher,
tänzerisch, klobig,
die Engels-
schwinge, schwer von Unsichtbarem, am
wundgeschundenen Fuß, kopf-
lastig getrimmt
vom Schwarzhagel, der
auch dort fiel, in Witebsk,

– und sie, die ihn säten, sie
schreiben ihn weg
mit mimetischer Panzerfaustklaue! –,

geht, geht umher,
sucht,
sucht unten,
sucht droben, fern, sucht
mit dem Auge, holt
Alpha Centauri herunter, Arktur, holt
den Strahl hinzu, aus den Gräbern,

TABERNACLE WINDOW

The eye, dark:
as tabernacle window. It gathers,
what was world, remains world: the migrant
East, the
hovering ones, the
human beings-and-Jews,
the people of clouds, magnetically
with heart-fingers, you
it attracts, Earth:
you are coming, coming,
we shall dwell at last, dwell, something

– a breath? a name? –

moves about over orphaned ground,
light as a dancer, cloddish,
the angel's
wing, heavy with what's invisible, on
the foot rubbed sore, trimmed
down by the head, with
the black hail that
fell there too, at Vitebsk,

– and those who sowed it, they
write it away with
a mimetic anti-tank claw! –

moves, moves about,
searches,
searches below,
searches above, far, searches
with eyes, fetches
Alpha Centauri down, and Arcturus, fetches
the ray as well, from the graves,

geht zu Ghetto und Eden, pflückt
das Sternbild zusammen, das er,
der Mensch, zum Wohnen braucht, hier,
unter Menschen,

schreitet
die Buchstaben ab und der Buchstaben sterblich-
unsterbliche Seele,
geht zu Aleph und Jud und geht weiter,

baut ihn, den Davidsschild, läßt ihn
aufflammen, einmal,

läßt ihn erlöschen – da steht er,
unsichtbar, steht
bei Alpha und Aleph, bei Jud,
bei den andern, bei
allen: in
dir,

Beth, – das ist
das Haus, wo der Tisch steht mit

dem Licht und dem Licht.

goes to ghetto and Eden, gathers
the constellation which they,
humankind, need for dwelling, here,
among humankind,

pacing,
musters the letters and the mortal-
immortal soul of letters,
goes to Aleph and Yod and goes farther,

builds it, the shield of David, and lets
it flare up, once,

lets it go out – there he stands,
invisible, stands
beside Alpha and Aleph, beside Yod
and the others, beside
everyone: in
you,

Beth, – that is
the house where the table stands with

the light and the Light.

Es ist alles anders, als du es dir denkst, als ich es mir denke,
die Fahne weht noch,
die kleinen Geheimnisse sind noch bei sich,
sie werfen noch Schatten, davon
lebst du, leb ich, leben wir.

Die Silbermünze auf deiner Zunge schmilzt,
sie schmeckt nach Morgen, nach Immer, ein Weg
nach Rußland steigt dir ins Herz,
die karelische Birke
hat
gewartet,
der Name Ossip kommt auf dich zu, du erzählst ihm,
was er schon weiß, er nimmt es, er nimmt es dir ab, mit Händen,
du löst ihm den Arm von der Schulter, den rechten, den linken,
du heftest die deinen an ihre Stelle, mit Händen, mit Fingern,
    mit Linien,

– was abriß, wächst wieder zusammen –
da hast du sie, da nimm sie dir, da hast du alle beide,
den Namen, den Namen, die Hand, die Hand,
da nimm sie dir zum Unterpfand,
er nimmt auch das, und du hast
wieder, was dein ist, was sein war,

Windmühlen

stoßen dir Luft in die Lunge, du ruderst
durch die Kanäle, Lagunen und Grachten,
bei Wortschein,
am Heck kein Warum, am Bug kein Wohin, ein Widderhorn
    hebt dich
– Tekiah! –
wie ein Posaunenschall über die Nächte hinweg in den Tag, die
    Auguren
zerfleischen einander, der Mensch

EVERYTHING'S DIFFERENT from how you conceive it, I conceive it,
the flag still flutters,
the little secrets are still all there,
they still cast shadows, by that
you live, I live, we live.

The silver coin on your tongue melts,
it tastes of morning, of Ever, a way
to Russia ascends to your heart,
the Karelian birch tree
has
waited,
the name Osip walks up to you, and you tell him
what he knows already, he takes, he accepts it from you, with
    hands,
you detach an arm from his shoulder, the right, the left,
you attach your own in its place, with hands, with fingers, with
    lines,

– what was severed joins up again –
there you have it, so take it, there you have them both,
the name, the name, the hand, the hand,
so take them, keep them as a pledge,
he takes it too, and you have
again what is yours, what was his,

windmills

push air into your lungs, you row
down the waterways, lagoons, Dutch canals,
by the light of words,
on the stern no why, on the bow no whither, a ram's horn lifts
    you
– *Tekiah!* –
like a trumpet blast over nights into day, the augurs
devour one another, man

hat seinen Frieden, der Gott
hat den seinen, die Liebe
kehrt in die Betten zurück, das Haar
der Frauen wächst wieder,
die nach innen gestülpte
Knospe an ihrer Brust
tritt wieder zutag, lebens-,
herzlinienhin erwacht sie
dir in der Hand, die den Lendenweg hochklomm, —

wie heißt es, dein Land
hinterm Berg, hinterm Jahr?
Ich weiß, wie es heißt.
Wie das Wintermärchen, so heißt es,
es heißt wie das Sommermärchen,
das Dreijahreland deiner Mutter, das war es,
das ists,
es wandert überallhin, wie die Sprache,
wirf sie weg, wirf sie weg,
dann hast du sie wieder, wie ihn,
den Kieselstein aus
der Mährischen Senke,
den dein Gedanke nach Prag trug,
aufs Grab, auf die Gräber, ins Leben,
längst
ist er fort, wie die Briefe, wie alle
Laternen, wieder
mußt du ihn suchen, da ist er,
klein ist er, weiß,
um die Ecke, da liegt er,
bei Normandie-Njemen – in Böhmen,
da, da, da,
hinterm Haus, vor dem Haus,
weiß ist er, weiß, er sagt:
Heute – es gilt.
Weiß ist er, weiß, ein Wasser-
strahl findet hindurch, ein Herzstrahl,
ein Fluß,

has his peace, God
has his, love
returns to the beds, the hair
of women grows again,
the retracted
bud on their breasts
emerges again, life –
heartlinewards it awakens
in your hand that climbed up the loinway, –

what is it called, your country
behind the mountain, behind the year?
I know what it's called.
Like the winter's tale, it is called,
it's called like the summer's tale,
your mother's threeyearland, that's what it was,
what it is,
it wanders off everywhere, like language,
throw it away, throw it away,
then you'll have it again, like that other thing,
the pebble from
the Moravian hollow
which your thought carried to Prague,
on to the grave, to the graves, into life,
long
now it has been gone, like the letters, like all
the lamps, once again
you must look for it, there it is,
a little thing, white,
round the corner, that's where it lies,
near Normandy-Niemen – in Bohemia,
there, there, there,
behind the house, in front of the house,
it's white, white, it says:
Today – that's what matters.
It's white, white, a water-
jet finds its way through, a heartjet,
a river,

du kennst seinen Namen, die Ufer
hängen voll Tag, wie der Name,
du tastest ihn ab, mit der Hand:
Alba.

you know its name, the banks
are laden with day, like the name,
you feel it out, with your hand:
Alba.

IN DER LUFT, da bleibt deine Wurzel, da,
in der Luft.
Wo sich das Irdische ballt, erdig,
Atem-und-Lehm.

Groß
geht der Verbannte dort oben, der
Verbrannte: ein Pommer, zuhause
im Maikäferlied, das mütterlich blieb, sommerlich, hell-
blütig am Rand
aller schroffen,
winterhart-kalten
Silben.

Mit ihm
wandern die Meridiane:
an-
gesogen von seinem
sonnengesteuerten Schmerz, der die Länder verbrüdert nach
dem Mittagsspruch einer
liebenden
Ferne. Aller-
orten ist Hier und ist Heute, ist, von Verzweiflungen her,
der Glanz,
in den die Entzweiten treten mit ihren
geblendeten Mündern:

der Kuß, nächtlich,
brennt einer Sprache den Sinn ein, zu der sie erwachen, sie —:

heimgekehrt in
den unheimlichen Bannstrahl,
der die Verstreuten versammelt, die
durch die Sternwüste Seele Geführten, die
Zeltmacher droben im Raum
ihrer Blicke und Schiffe,
die winzigen Garben Hoffnung,
darin es von Erzengelfittichen rauscht, von Verhängnis,
die Brüder, die Schwestern, die

IN THE AIR, that's where your root remains, there,
in the air.
Where the terrestrial rounds itself, clenched, earthy,
both breath and clay.

Unbowed
the banished walks up there, the
branded, burnt: a man from Pommern, at home
in the cockchafer song, still motherly, summery, bright-
blooded at the rim
of all the harsh,
winter-hard-chilling
syllables.

Together with him
the meridians wander:
sucked
in by his
sun-steered pain that makes brothers of countries under
the noonday spell of a
loving
distance. Every-
where is Here and Today, by dint of despairs is
the radiance
into which the divided step with their
blinded mouths:

the kiss, nocturnal,
into a language brands the meaning they wake to, they –:

come home into
the uncanny banishment ray
that gathers the scattered, those
led through the star desert soul, the
tent-makers up in the space
of their gazing and ships,
the tiny sheaves of hope
in which there's a swish of archangels' wings, of doom,
the brothers, the sisters found

zu leicht, die zu schwer, die zu leicht
Befundenen mit
der Weltenwaage im blut-
schändrischen, im
fruchtbaren Schoß, die lebenslang Fremden,
spermatisch bekränzt von Gestirnen, schwer
in den Untiefen lagernd, die Leiber
zu Schwellen getürmt, zu Dämmen, – die

Furtenwesen, darüber
der Klumpfuß der Götter herüber-
gestolpert kommt – um
wessen
Sternzeit zu spät?

too light, too heavy, too light
on the scale of the worlds in the in-
cestuous, in the
fruitful womb, those life-long aliens
spermatically wreathed with constellations, heavily
encamped in the shallows, their bodies
piled up into thresholds, embankments, – those

ford creatures over which
the club-footed god comes
stumbling across – by
whose
stellar time too late?

FROM
Atemwende
(1967)

STEHEN im Schatten
des Wundenmals in der Luft.

Für-niemand-und-nichts-Stehn.
Unerkannt,
für dich
allein.

Mit allem, was darin Raum hat,
auch ohne
Sprache.

MIT DEN VERFOLGTEN in spätem, un-
verschwiegenem,
strahlendem
Bund.

Das Morgen-Lot, übergoldet,
heftet sich dir an die mit-
schwörende, mit-
schürfende, mit-
schreibende
Ferse.

To STAND in the shadow
of the scar up in the air.

To stand-for-no-one-and-nothing.
Unrecognized,
for you
alone.

With all there is room for in that,
even without
language.

PLEDGED TO THE PERSECUTED, by
a late, un-
tacit, luminous
bond.

The morning's plumb lead, gilded,
affixes itself to your co-
vowing, co-
prospecting, co-
writing
heel.

FADENSONNEN
über der grauschwarzen Ödnis.
Ein baum-
hoher Gedanke
greift sich den Lichtton: es sind
noch Lieder zu singen jenseits
der Menschen.

IM SCHLANGENWAGEN, an
der weißen Zypresse vorbei,
durch die Flut
fuhren sie dich.

Doch in dir, von
Geburt,
schäumte die andre Quelle,
am schwarzen
Strahl Gedächtnis
klommst du zutag.

THREAD SUNS
above the grey-black wilderness.
A tree-
high thought
tunes in to light's pitch: there áre
still songs to be sung on the other side
of mankind.

IN THE SNAKE CARRIAGE, past
the white cypress tree,
through the surge
they drove you.

But in you, from
birth,
the other wellspring foamed,
on the black
jet remembrance
dayward you climbed.

WORTAUFSCHÜTTUNG, vulkanisch,
meerüberrauscht.

Oben
der flutende Mob
der Gegengeschöpfe: er
flaggte – Abbild und Nachbild
kreuzen eitel zeithin.

Bis du den Wortmond hinaus-
schleuderst, von dem her
das Wunder Ebbe geschieht
und der herz-
förmige Krater
nackt für die Anfänge zeugt,
die Königs-
geburten.

PILING-ON OF WORDS, volcanic,
drowned by the sea's roar.

Above,
the surging mob
of anti-creatures: it
hoisted flags — image and copy
vainly cruise timeward.

Till you hurl forth the
word-moon that makes
the ebb-tide's miracle happen
and that creates
heart-
shaped craters, bare for beginnings,
for kingly
births.

WEGGEBEIZT vom
Strahlenwind deiner Sprache
das bunte Gerede des An-
erlebten – das hundert-
züngige Mein-
gedicht, das Genicht.

Aus-
gewirbelt,
frei
der Weg durch den menschen-
gestaltigen Schnee,
den Büßerschnee, zu
den gastlichen
Gletscherstuben und -tischen.

Tief
in der Zeitenschrunde,
beim
Wabeneis
wartet, ein Atemkristall,
dein unumstößliches
Zeugnis.

ETCHED AWAY from
the ray-shot wind of your language
the garish talk of rubbed-
off experience – the hundred-
tongued pseudo-
poem, the noem.

Whirled
clear,
free
your way through the human-
shaped snow,
the penitents' snow, to
the hospitable
glacier rooms and tables.

Deep
in Time's crevasse
by
the alveolate ice
waits, a crystal of breath,
your irreversible
witness.

KEINE SANDKUNST MEHR, kein Sandbuch, keine Meister.

Nichts erwürfelt. Wieviel
Stumme?
Siebenzehn.

Deine Frage – deine Antwort.
Dein Gesang, was weiß er?

Tiefimschnee,
            Iefimnee,
                      I – i – e.

No more sand art, no sand book, no masters.

Nothing won by dicing. How many
dumb ones?
Seventeen.

Your question – your answer.
Your song, what does it know?

Deepinsnow,
        Eepinnow,
                Ee – i – o.

ALS UNS DAS WEISSE ANFIEL, nachts;
als aus dem Spendekrug mehr
kam als Wasser;
als das geschundene Knie
der Opferglocke den Wink gab:
Flieg! –

Da
war ich
noch ganz.

HOHLES LEBENSGEHÖFT. Im Windfang
die leer-
geblasene Lunge
blüht. Eine Handvoll
Schlafkorn
weht aus dem wahr-
gestammelten Mund
hinaus zu den Schnee-
gesprächen.

WHEN WHITENESS ATTACKED US, at night;
when from the alms jug flowed
more than water;
when the flayed knee
gave this hint to the offertory bell:
Fly! –

Then
I was
whole still.

HOLLOW HOMESTEAD OF LIFE. In the porch
the lung
blown empty
blossoms. A handful
of sleep grain
wafts from the mouth
stammered true,
out to the snow
conversations.

AM WEISSEN GEBETRIEMEN – der
Herr dieser Stunde
war
ein Wintergeschöpf, ihm
zulieb
geschah, was geschah –
biß sich mein kletternder Mund fest, noch einmal,
als er dich suchte, Rauchspur
du, droben,
in Frauengestalt,
du auf der Reise zu meinen
Feuergedanken im Schwarzkies
jenseits der Spaltworte, durch
die ich dich gehn sah, hoch-
beinig und
den schwerlippigen eignen
Kopf
auf dem von meinen
tödlich genauen
Händen
lebendigen Körper.

Sag deinen dich
bis in die Schluchten hinein-
begleitenden Fingern, wie
ich dich kannte, wie weit
ich dich ins Tiefe stieß, wo
dich mein bitterster Traum
herzher beschlief, im Bett
meines unablösbaren Namens.

ON THE WHITE PRAYER-THONG – the
Lord of this hour
was
a winter creature, for
his sake
happened what happened –
my climbing mouth bit and locked, once again,
looking for you, smoke trail
above me, you,
in the shape of a woman,
you on your way to my
fire thoughts in the black shingle
on the other side of dividing words, through
which I saw you walk, long-
legged and
your thick-lipped own
head
on my body
alive
by dint of my deadly
accurate hands.

Tell your fingers that
accompany you down into
chasms even, how
I knew you, how far
I pushed you into the deep, where
my most bitter dream
slept with you from the heart, in the bed
of my undetachable name.

ERBLINDE schon heut:
auch die Ewigkeit steht voller Augen –
darin
ertrinkt, was den Bildern hinweghalf
über den Weg, den sie kamen,
darin
erlischt, was auch dich aus der Sprache
fortnahm mit einer Geste,
die du geschehn ließt wie
den Tanz zweier Worte aus lauter
Herbst und Seide und Nichts.

UNTER DIE HAUT meiner Hände genäht:
dein mit Händen
getrösteter Name.

Wenn ich den Klumpen Luft
knete, unsere Nahrung,
säuert ihn der
Buchstabenschimmer aus
der wahnwitzig-offenen
Pore.

GO BLIND now, today:
eternity also is full of eyes —
in them
drowns what helped images down
the way they came,
in them
fades what took you out of language,
lifted you out with a gesture
which you allowed to happen like
the dance of the words made of
autumn and silk and nothingness.

SEWN UNDER THE SKIN of my hands:
your name
that hands comforted.

When I knead the
lump of air, our nourishment,
it is soured by
the letter effulgence from
the dementedly open
pore.

SCHWARZ,
wie die Erinnerungswunde,
wühlen die Augen nach dir
in dem von Herzzähnen hell-
gebissenen Kronland,
das unser Bett bleibt:

durch diesen Schacht mußt du kommen –
du kommst.

Im Samen-
sinn
sternt dich das Meer aus, zuinnerst, für immer.

Das Namengeben hat ein Ende,
über dich werf ich mein Schicksal.

BLACK
as memory's wound
the eyes root for you
in this plot bitten
bright by the heart-teeth,
crownland that remains our bed:

through this shaft you must come –
you come.

In the seminal
sense
the sea stars you out, inmostly, for ever.

There's an end to the giving of names,
over you I cast my fate.

LANDSCHAFT mit Urnenwesen.
Gespräche
von Rauchmund zu Rauchmund.

Sie essen:
die Tollhäusler-Trüffel, ein Stück
unvergrabner Poesie,
fand Zunge und Zahn.

Eine Träne rollt in ihr Auge zurück.

Die linke, verwaiste
Hälfte der Pilger-
muschel – sie schenkten sie dir,
dann banden sie dich –
leuchtet lauschend den Raum aus:

das Klinkerspiel gegen den Tod
kann beginnen.

LANDSCAPE with urn creatures.
Conversations
from smoke mouth to smoke mouth.

They eat:
those madhouse truffles, a chunk
of unburied poetry,
found a tongue and a tooth.

A tear rolls back into its eye.

The left-hand, orphaned
half of the pilgrim's
shell – they gave it to you,
then they fettered you –
listening, floodlights the scene:

the clinker game against death
can begin.

DIE GAUKLERTROMMEL,
von meinem Herzgroschen laut.

Die Sprossen der Leiter, über
die Odysseus, mein Affe, nach Ithaka klettert,
rue de Longchamp, eine Stunde
nach dem verschütteten Wein:

tu das zum Bild,
das uns heimwürfelt in
den Becher, in dem ich bei dir lieg,
unausspielbar.

THE JUGGLER'S DRUM
loud with my heart's penny.

The rungs of that ladder on which
Odysseus, my monkey, clambers to Ithaca,
rue de Longchamps, one hour
after the spilled wine:

add that to the picture
that dices us home into
the cup in which I lie with you,
uncastable.

WENN DU IM BETT
aus verschollenem Fahnentuch liegst,
bei blauschwarzen Silben, im Schneewimperschatten,
kommt, durch Gedanken-
güsse,
der Kranich geschwommen, stählern –
du öffnest dich ihm.

Sein Schnabel tickt dir die Stunde
in jeden Mund – in jeder
glöcknert, mit glutrotem Strang, ein Schweige-
Jahrtausend,
Unfrist und Frist
münzen einander zutode,
die Taler, die Groschen
regnen dir hart durch die Poren,
in
Sekundengestalt
fliegst du hin und verrammelst
die Türen Gestern und Morgen, – phosphorn,
wie Ewigkeitszähne,
knospt deine eine, knospt auch die
andere Brust,
den Griffen entgegen, unter
den Stößen –: so dicht,
so tief
gestreut
ist der sternige
Kranich-
Same.

WHEN YOU LIE in
the bed of lost flag cloth,
with blue-black syllables, in snow eyelash shade,
through thought-
showers
the crane comes gliding, steely –
you open to him.

His bill ticks the hour for you
into every mouth – in each hour,
with a red-hot rope, bell-rings a
millennium of silence,
unrespite and respite
mint each other to death,
the florins, the pennies
rain hard through your pores,
in
the shape of seconds
you fly there and bar
the doors yesterday and tomorrow, – phosphorescent,
like eternity teeth,
your one breast buds, and the other
breast buds too,
towards the graspings, under
the thrusts –: so densely,
so deeply
strewn
is the starry
crane-
seed.

IN PRAG

Der halbe Tod,
großgesäugt mit unserm Leben,
lag aschenbildwahr um uns her –

auch wir
tranken noch immer, seelenverkreuzt, zwei Degen,
an Himmelssteine genäht, wortblutgeboren
im Nachtbett,

größer und größer
wuchsen wir durcheinander, es gab
keinen Namen mehr für
das, was uns trieb (einer der Wieviel-
unddreißig
war mein lebendiger Schatten,
der die Wahnstiege hochklomm zu dir?),

ein Turm,
baute der Halbe sich ins Wohin,
ein Hradschin
aus lauter Goldmacher-Nein,

Knochen-Hebräisch,
zu Sperma zermahlen,
rann durch die Sanduhr,
die wir durchschwammen, zwei Träume jetzt, läutend
wider die Zeit, auf den Plätzen.

IN PRAGUE

That half-death,
suckled big with our life,
lay around us, true as an ashen image –

we too
still drank, soul-crossed, two daggers,
sewn on to stones of the sky, born of word blood
in the night bed,

bigger and bigger
we grew interlaced, there was
no longer a name for
that which drove us (one of the how many
and thirty
was my live shadow
that climbed the delusory steps towards you?),

a tower
the halved one built for himself into where,
a Hradshin
made of pure gold-makers' No,

bone-Hebrew
ground into sperm
ran through the hourglass
through which we swam, two dreams now, chiming
against time, in the squares.

DAS GESCHRIEBENE höhlt sich, das
Gesprochene, meergrün,
brennt in den Buchten,

in den
verflüssigten Namen
schnellen die Tümmler,

im geewigten Nirgends, hier,
im Gedächtnis der über-
lauten Glocken in – wo nur?,

wer
in diesem
Schattengeviert
schnaubt, wer
unter ihm
schimmert auf, schimmert auf, schimmert auf?

THAT WHICH WAS WRITTEN grows hollow, that
which was spoken, sea-green,
burns in the coves,

in the
liquidized names
the porpoises leap,

in the eternalized Nowhere, here,
in recollection of the too-
loud bells in – but where?,

who
in this
shadow square
snorts, who
beneath it
shines out, shines out, shines out?

CELLO-EINSATZ
von hinter dem Schmerz:

die Gewalten, nach Gegen-
himmeln gestaffelt,
wälzen Undeutbares vor
Einflugschneise und Einfahrt,

der
erklommene Abend
steht voller Lungengeäst,

zwei
Brandwolken Atem
graben im Buch,
das der Schläfenlärm aufschlug,

etwas wird wahr,

zwölfmal erglüht
das von Pfeilen getroffene Drüben,

die Schwarz-
blütige trinkt
des Schwarzblütigen Samen,

alles ist weniger, als
es ist,
alles ist mehr.

CELLO ENTRY
from behind pain:

the powers, graded
towards counter-heavens,
roll out indecipherable things
in front of arrival runway and drive,

the
climbed evening
is thick with lung-scrub,

two
smoke-clouds of breath
dig in the book
which the temple-din opened,

something grows true,

twelve times the
beyond hit by arrows lights up,

the black-
blooded woman drinks
the black-blooded man's semen,

all things are less than
they are,
all are more.

KÖNIGSWUT, steinmähnig, vorn.

Und die verrauchten
Gebete –
Hengste, hinzu-
geschmerzt, die
unbezähmbar-gehorsame
Freischar:

psalmhufig, hinsingend über
auf-, auf-, auf-
geblättertes Bibelgebirg,
auf die klaren, mit-
klirrenden,
mächtigen Meerkeime zu.

KING'S RAGE, stony-maned, at the front.

And the prayers
risen as smoke –
stallions, a bonus of
anguish, that
untamable-compliant
army of volunteers:

psalm-hooved, singing their way over
Bible ranges flicked
open, open, open,
making for those
clear, co-
resonantly tinkling
mighty germs of seas.

SOLVE

Entosteter, zu
Brandscheiten zer-
spaltener Grabbaum:

an den Gift-
pfalzen vorbei, an den Domen,
stromaufwärts, strom-
abwärts geflößt

vom winzig-lodernden, vom
freien
Satzzeichen der
zu den unzähligen zu
nennenden un-
aussprechlichen
Namen aus-
einandergeflohenen, ge-
borgenen
Schrift.

SOLVE

De-Eastered, grave-
tree split into
logs for burning:

past the poison-
palatinates, past the cathedrals,
floated upstream,
downstream

by the tinily flaring, the
free punctuation marks of
the sequestered writ that
has dis-
persed
into the
countless, un-
utterable,
to be uttered
names.

COAGULA

Auch deine
Wunde, Rosa.

Und das Hörnerlicht deiner
rumänischen Büffel
an Sternes Statt überm
Sandbett, im
redenden, rot-
aschengewaltigen
Kolben.

COAGULA

And your wound
also, Rosa.

And the hornlight of your
Romanian buffaloes
instead of stars above
the sandbed, in
the vociferous, red-
ashes-powerful
retort.

OSTERQUALM, flutend, mit
der buchstabenähnlichen
Kielspur inmitten.

(Niemals war Himmel.
Doch Meer ist noch, brandrot,
Meer.)

Wir hier, wir,
überfahrtsfroh, vor dem Zelt,
wo du Wüstenbrot bukst
aus mitgewanderter Sprache.

Am äußersten Blickrand: der Tanz
zweier Klingen übers
Herzschattenseil.

Das Netz darunter, geknüpft
aus Gedanken-
enden – in welcher
Tiefe?

Da: der zerbissene
Ewigkeitsgroschen, zu uns
heraufgespien durch die Maschen.

Drei Sandstimmen, drei
Skorpione:
das Gastvolk, mit uns
im Kahn.

THICK EASTER SMOKE, flowing, with
the letter-like
wake in the midst.

(Sky never was.
But there is sea still, flame-red,
sea.)

We here, we,
passage-happy, in front of the tent
where you baked desert bread
out of camp-following language.

At the outermost edge of vision: the dance
of two blades
across the heart-shadow-rope.

Beneath it, the net, knotted
out of thought-
ends – at what
depth?

There: the bitten-through
eternity penny, spewed
up to us through the meshes.

Three sand voices, three
scorpions:
the visiting folk, with us
in the boat.

EIN DRÖHNEN: es ist
die Wahrheit selbst
unter die Menschen
getreten,
mitten ins
Metapherngestöber.

A RUMBLING: truth
itself has appeared
among humankind
in the very thick of their
flurrying metaphors.

Ins Hirn gehaun – halb? zu drei Vierteln? –,
gibst du, genächtet, die Parolen – diese:

»Tatarenpfeile«.
          »Kunstbrei«.
               »Atem«.

Es kommen alle, keiner fehlt und keine.
(Sipheten und Probyllen sind dabei.)

Es kommt ein Mensch.

Weltapfelgroß die Träne neben dir,
durchrauscht, durchfahren
von Antwort,
          Antwort,
              Antwort.
Durcheist – von wem?

»Passiert«, sagst du,
          »passiert«,
              »passiert«.

Der stille Aussatz löst sich dir vom Gaumen
und fächelt deiner Zunge Licht zu,
              Licht.

GIVE THE WORD

Cut to the brain – half? by three quarters? –,
nighted, you give the passwords – these:

"Tartars' arrows."
                    "Art pap."
                                "Breath."

All come. Male or female, not one is missing.
(Siphets and probyls among them.)

A human being comes.

World-apple-sized the tear beside you,
roared through, rushed through
by answer,
            answer,
                    answer.
Iced through – by whom?

"Pass" you say,
                "pass",
                        "pass".

The quiet scab works free from off your palate
and fanwise at your tongue blows light,
                                        blows light.

GROSSE, GLÜHENDE WÖLBUNG
mit dem sich
hinaus- und hinweg-
wühlenden Schwarzgestirn-Schwarm:

der verkieselten Stirn eines Widders
brenn ich dies Bild ein, zwischen
die Hörner, darin,
im Gesang der Windungen, das
Mark der geronnenen
Herzmeere schwillt.

Wo-
gegen
rennt er nicht an?

Die Welt ist fort, ich muß dich tragen.

VAST, GLOWING VAULT
with the swarm of
black stars pushing them-
selves out and away:

on to a ram's silicified forehead.
I brand this image, between
the horns, in which,
in the song of the whorls, the
marrow of melted
heart-oceans swells.

In-
to what
does he not charge?

The world is gone, I must carry you.

DUNSTBÄNDER-, SPRUCHBÄNDER-AUFSTAND,
röter als rot,
während der großen
Frostschübe, auf
schlitternden Eisbuckeln, vor
Robbenvölkern.

Der durch dich hindurch-
gehämmerte Strahl,
der hier schreibt,
röter als rot.

Mit seinen Worten
dich aus der Hirnschale schälen, hier,
verscharrter Oktober.

Mit dir das Gold prägen, jetzt,
wenns herausstirbt.

Mit dir den Bändern beistehn.

Mit dir das glasharte Flugblatt vertäuen
am lesenden Blutpoller, den
die Erde durch diesen
Stiefpol hinausstieß.

UPRISING OF SMOKE BANNERS, WORD BANNERS,
redder than red,
during the great
frost waves, on
sliding icehumps, in front of
seal peoples.

The ray hammered
through you
that writes here,
redder than red.

Use its words
to peel from your cranium, here,
you, buried October.

Use you to mint the gold, now,
as it dies its way out.

Use you to come to the banners' aid.

Use you to moor the glasshard leaflet
to the reading blood bollard which
through this step-pole
earth pushed out.

EINMAL,
da hörte ich ihn,
da wusch er die Welt,
ungesehn, nachtlang,
wirklich.

Eins und Unendlich,
vernichtet,
ichten.

Licht war. Rettung.

Once
I heard him,
he was washing the world,
unseen, nightlong,
real.

One and Infinite,
annihilated,
ied.

Light was. Salvation.

FROM
Fadensonnen
(1968)

Du warst mein Tod:
dich konnte ich halten,
während mir alles entfiel.

Zur Rechten – wer? Die Tödin.
Und du, zur Linken, du?

Die Reise-Sicheln am außer-
himmlischen Ort
mimen sich weißgrau
zu Mondschwalben zusammen,
zu Sternmauerseglern,

ich tauche dorthin
und gieß eine Urnevoll
in dich hinunter,
hinein.

YOU WERE my death:
you I could hold
when all fell away from me.

TO MY RIGHT – who? The deathwoman.
And you, to my left, you?

The travelling-sickles at the extra-
celestial place
mime themselves whitish-grey
into moon swallows,
into star swifts,

I dip to that place
and pour an urnful
down you,
into you.

MÖWENKÜKEN, silbern,
betteln den Altvogel an:
den Rotfleck am Unter-
schnabel, der gelb ist.

Schwarz – eine Kopf-
attrappe führt es dir vor –
wär ein stärkerer Reiz. Auch Blau
ist wirksam, doch nicht
die Reizfarbe machts:
es muß eine
Reizgestalt sein, eine ganze,
komplett
konfiguriert,
ein vorgegebenes Erbe.

. . . .

Freund,
teerübergoßner Sackhüpfer du,
auch hier, auf diesem
Gestade gerätst du
beiden, Zeit und Ewigkeit, in die
falsche
Kehle.

GULL CHICKS, silvery,
solicit the adult bird:
with the red spot on the lower
beak that is yellow.

Black – a dummy
head demonstrates it to you –
would be a stronger stimulus. Blue
is also effective, but
the colour is not what does it:
it has to be
a stimulus shape, a whole one,
completely
configured,
a pre-dated inheritance.

. . . .

Friend,
you tar-covered sack-race hopper,
here too, on this
shore, in both, in
time's and eternity's gullets, you go
down
the wrong way.

IRISCH

Gib mir das Wegrecht
über die Kornstiege zu deinem Schlaf,
das Wegrecht
über den Schlafpfad,
das Recht, daß ich Torf stechen kann
am Herzhang,
morgen.

TAU. Und ich lag mit dir, du, im Gemülle,
ein matschiger Mond
bewarf uns mit Antwort,

wir bröckelten auseinander
und bröselten wieder in eins:

der Herr brach das Brot,
das Brot brach den Herrn.

IRISH

Give me the right of way
over the corn steps into your sleep,
the right of way
over the sleep path,
the right to cut peat
on the heart slope,
tomorrow.

DEW. And I lay with you, you, amid garbage,
a mushy moon
pelted us with answers,

we crumbled apart
and crumbled into one again:

the Lord broke the bread,
the bread broke the Lord.

... AUCH KEINERLEI
Friede.

Graunächte, vorbewußt-kühl.
Reizmengen, otterhaft,
auf Bewußtseinsschotter
unterwegs zu
Erinnerungsbläschen.

Grau-in-Grau der Substanz.

Ein Halbschmerz, ein zweiter, ohne
Dauerspur, halbwegs
hier. Eine Halblust.
Bewegtes, Besetztes.

Wiederholungszwangs-
Camaïeu.

MÄCHTE, GEWALTEN.

Dahinter, im Bambus:
bellende Lepra, symphonisch.

Vincents verschenktes
Ohr
ist am Ziel.

... AND NO KIND OF
peace.

Grey nights, foreknown to be cool.
Stimulus dollops, otter-like,
over consciousness gravel
on their way to
little memory bubbles.

Grey-within-grey of substance.

A half-pain, a second one, with no
lasting trace, half-way
here. A half-desire.
Things in motion, things occupied.

Cameo
of compulsive repetition.

POWERS, DOMINIONS

Behind them, in the bamboo:
barking leprosy, symphonic.

Vincent's posted
ear
has reached its destination.

DENK DIR

Denk dir:
der Moorsoldat von Massada
bringt sich Heimat bei, aufs
unauslöschlichste,
wider
allen Dorn im Draht.

Denk dir:
die Augenlosen ohne Gestalt
führen dich frei durchs Gewühl, du
erstarkst und
erstarkst.

Denk dir: deine
eigene Hand
hat dies wieder
ins Leben empor-
gelittene
Stück
bewohnbarer Erde
gehalten.

Denk dir:
das kam auf mich zu,
namenwach, handwach
für immer,
vom Unbestattbaren her.

THINK OF IT

Think of it:
the bog soldier of Massada
teaches himself home, most
inextinguishably,
against
every barb in the wire.

Think of it:
the eyeless with no shape
lead you free through the tumult, you
grow stronger and
stronger.

Think of it: your
own hand
has held
this bit of
habitable
earth, suffered up
again
into life.

Think of it:
this came towards me,
name-awake, hand-awake
for ever,
from the unburiable.

THINK OF IT

Think of it:
the boy soldier of Masada
teaches himself being, must
more deliberately,
against
every barb in the wire.

Think of it:
the eyeless with no shape
lead you free through the tunnel, you
grow another and
stronger.

Think of it: your
own hand
has held
this bit of
habitable
earth, suffered up
again
into life.

Think of it:
this came towards me,
name-awake, hand-awake
for ever,
from the unhabitable.

FROM
Lichtzwang
(1970)

HÖRRESTE, SEHRESTE, im
Schlafsaal eintausendundeins,

tagnächtlich
die Bären-Polka:

sie schulen dich um,

du wirst wieder
er.

IHN RITT DIE NACHT, er war zu sich gekommen,
der Waisenkittel war die Fahn,

kein Irrlauf mehr,
es ritt ihn grad –

Es ist, es ist, als stünden im Liguster die Orangen,
als hätt der so Gerittene nichts an
als seine
erste
muttermalige, ge-
heimnisgesprenkelte
Haut.

SCRAPS OF HEARD, OF SEEN THINGS, in
Ward a thousand and one,

day-nightly
the Bear Polka:

you're being re-educated,

they'll turn you back into
he.

NIGHT RODE HIM, he had come to his senses,
the orphan's tunic was his flag,

no more going astray,
it rode him straight –

It is, it is as though oranges hung in the privet,
as though the so-ridden had nothing on
but his
first
birth-marked, se-
cret-speckled
skin.

MIT MIKROLITHEN gespickte
schenkend-verschenkte
Hände.

Das Gespräch, das sich spinnt
von Spitze zu Spitze,
angesengt von
sprühender Brandluft.

Ein Zeichen
kämmt es zusammen
zur Antwort auf eine
grübelnde Felskunst.

WIR LAGEN
schon tief in der Macchia, als du
endlich herankrochst.
Doch konnten wir nicht
hinüberdunkeln zu dir:
es herrschte
Lichtzwang.

HANDS
giving – given away,
larded with microliths.

The conversation that's spun
from peak to peak,
scorched by
spume air from a fire.

A sign
combs it together
in reply to a
brain-racking rock art.

WE WERE LYING
deep in the macchia, by the time
you crept up at last.
But we could not
darken over to you:
light compulsion
reigned.

Was uns
zusammenwarf,
schrickt auseinander,

ein Weltstein, sonnenfern,
summt.

BEI BRANCUSI, ZU ZWEIT

Wenn dieser Steine einer
verlauten ließe,
was ihn verschweigt:
hier, nahebei,
am Humpelstock dieses Alten,
tät es sich auf, als Wunde,
in die du zu tauchen hättst,
einsam,
fern meinem Schrei, dem schon mit-
behauenen, weißen.

THAT WHICH
threw us together
startles apart,

a world-boulder, sun-remote,
hums.

AT BRANCUSI'S, THE TWO OF US

If one of these stones
were to give away
what it is that keeps silent about it:
here, nearby,
at this old man's limping stick,
it would open up, as a wound,
in which you would have to submerge,
lonely,
far from my scream, that is
chiselled already, white.

TODTNAUBERG

Arnika, Augentrost, der
Trunk aus dem Brunnen mit dem
Sternwürfel drauf,

in der
Hütte,

die in das Buch
– wessen Namen nahms auf
vor dem meinen? –,
die in dies Buch
geschriebene Zeile von
einer Hoffnung, heute,
auf eines Denkenden
kommendes
Wort
im Herzen,

Waldwasen, uneingeebnet,
Orchis und Orchis, einzeln,

Krudes, später, im Fahren,
deutlich,

der uns fährt, der Mensch,
der's mit anhört,

die halb-
beschrittenen Knüppel-
pfade im Hochmoor,

Feuchtes,
viel.

TODTNAUBERG

Arnica, eyebright, the
draft from the well with the
star-crowned die above it,

in the
hut,

the line
– whose name did the book
register before mine? –,
the line inscribed
in that book about
a hope, today,
of a thinking man's
coming
word
in the heart,

woodland sward, unlevelled,
orchid and orchid, single,

coarse stuff, later, clear
in passing,

he who drives us, the man,
who listens in,

the half-
trodden fascine
walks over the high moors,

dampness,
much.

JETZT, da die Betschemel brennen,
eß ich das Buch
mit allen
Insignien.

EINEM BRUDER IN ASIEN

Die selbstverklärten
Geschütze
fahren gen Himmel,

zehn
Bomber gähnen,

ein Schnellfeuer blüht,
so gewiß wie der Frieden,

eine Handvoll Reis
erstirbt als dein Freund.

Now that the hassocks are burning
I eat the book
with all its
insignia.

FOR A BROTHER IN ASIA

The self-transfigured
guns
ascend to heaven,

ten
bombers yawn,

a quick-firing flowers,
certain as peace,

a handful of rice
unto death remains your true friend.

WIE DU dich ausstirbst in mir:

noch im letzten
zerschlissenen
Knoten Atems
steckst du mit einem
Splitter
Leben.

HIGHGATE

Es geht ein Engel durch die Stube –:
du, dem unaufgeschlagenen Buch nah,
sprichst mich
wiederum los.

Zweimal findet das Heidekraut Nahrung.
Zweimal erblaßts.

How YOU die out in me:

down to the last
worn-out
knot of breath
you're there, with a
splinter
of life.

HIGHGATE

An angel has walked through the room –:
you, near the unopened book,
acquit
me once more.

Twice the heather finds nourishment.
Twice it fades.

ICH KANN DICH NOCH SEHN: ein Echo,
ertastbar mit Fühl-
wörtern, am Abschieds-
grat.

Dein Gesicht scheut leise,
wenn es auf einmal
lampenhaft hell wird
in mir, an der Stelle,
wo man am schmerzlichsten Nie sagt.

DIE EWIGKEITEN fuhren
ihm ins Gesicht und drüber
hinaus,

langsam löschte ein Brand
alles Gekerzte,

ein Grün, nicht von hier,
umflaumte das Kinn
des Steins, den die Waisen
begruben und wieder
begruben.

I CAN STILL SEE YOU: an echo
that can be groped towards with antenna
words, on the ridge of
parting.

Your face quietly shies
when suddenly
there is lamplike brightness
inside me, just at the point
where most painfully one says, never.

THE ETERNITIES struck
at his face and
past it,

slowly a conflagration extinguished
all candled things,

a green, not of this place,
with down covered the chin
of the rock which the orphans
buried and
buried again.

DIE IRIN, die abschiedsgefleckte,
beliest deine Hand,
schneller als
schnell.

Ihrer Blicke Bläue durchwächst sie,
Verlust und Gewinn
in einem:

du,
augenfingrige
Ferne.

KEIN HALBHOLZ mehr, hier,
in den Gipfelhängen,
kein mit-
sprechender
Thymian.

Grenzschnee und sein
die Pfähle und deren
Wegweiser-Schatten
aushorchender, tot-
sagender
Duft.

THE IRISHWOMAN, mottled with parting,
reads in your hand,
faster than
fast.

The blue of her glances grows through her,
loss and gain
in one:

you,
eye-fingered
farness.

NO MORE HALF-WOOD, here,
on the summit slopes,
no col-
loquial
thyme.

Border snow and
its odour that
auscultates the posts and
their road-sign shadows,
declaring them
dead.

Mir wuchs Zinn in die Hand,
ich wußte mir nicht
zu helfen:
modeln mochte ich nicht,
lesen mocht es mich nicht –

Wenn sich jetzt
Ossietzkys letzte
Trinkschale fände,
ließ ich das Zinn
von ihr lernen,

und das Heer der Pilger-
stäbe
durchschwiege, durchstünde die Stunde.

ORANIENSTRASSE 1

Tin grew into my hand,
I did not know
what to do:
I had no wish to model,
it had no wish to read me –

If now
Ossietzky's last
drinking cup were found
I should let the tin
learn from that,

and the host of pilgrim
staves
would stone-wall, withstand the hour.

BRUNNEN-
artig
ins Verwunschne getieft,
mit doppelt gewalmten
Tagträumen drüber,

Quader-
ringe
um jeden Hauch:

die Kammer, wo ich dich ließ, hockend,
dich zu behalten,

das Herz befehligt
den uns leise bestrickenden Frost
an den geschiedenen
Fronten,

du wirst keine Blume sein
auf Urnenfeldern
und mich, den Schriftträger, holt
kein Erz aus der runden
Holz-Lehm-Hütte, kein
Engel.

SUBMERGED
well-
like into accursedness,
with doubly hipped
daydreams above,

ashlar
rings
around each breath:

the bedroom where I left you, crouching
so as to hold you,

the heart commands
the frost that gently captivates us
on the divided
fronts,

you will be no flower
on urn fields
and me, the script-bearer, no
ore releases from the round
wood and mud cabin, no
angel.

FAHLSTIMMIG, aus
der Tiefe geschunden:
kein Wort, kein Ding,
und beider einziger Name,

fallgerecht in dir,
fluggerecht in dir,

wunder Gewinn
einer Welt.

FALLOW-VOICED, lashed
forth from the depth:
no word, no thing,
and either's unique name,

primed in you for falling,
primed in you for flying,

sore gain
of a world.

SPERRIGES MORGEN
ich beiße mich in dich, ich schweige mich an dich,

wir tönen,
allein,

pastos
vertropfen die Ewigkeitsklänge,
durchquäkt
von heutigem
Gestern,

wir fahren,

groß
nimmt uns der letzte
Schallbecher auf:

den beschleunigten Herzschritt
draußen
im Raum,
bei ihr, der Erd-
achse.

OBSTRUCTIVE TOMORROW
I bite my way into you, my silence nestles into you,

we sound,
alone,

pastily
eternity's tones drip away,
croaked through by
the hodiernal
yesterday,

we travel,

largely
the last of the sonic bowls
receives us:

the boosted heart pace
outside
in space,
brought home to the axis
of Earth.

STREU OCKER in meine Augen:
du lebst nicht
mehr drin,

spar
mit Grab-
beigaben, spar,

schreite die Steinreihen ab,
auf den Händen,

mit ihrem Traum
streich über die
ausgemünzte
Schläfenbeinschuppe,

an der
großen
Gabelung er-
zähl dich dem Ocker
dreimal, neunmal.

SPRINKLE OCHRE into my eyes:
no longer
you live in them,

be sparing,
of graveside
supplements, be sparing,

walk up and down the stone rows
on your hands,

with their dream
graze the debased coinage,
the scale of
my temporal bone,

at the
great
road fork tell
yourself to the ochre
three times, nine times.

SCHALTJAHRHUNDERTE, Schalt-
sekunden, Schalt-
geburten, novembernd, Schalt-
tode,

in Wabentrögen gespeichert,
bits
on chips,

das Menoragedicht aus Berlin,

(Unasyliert, un-
archiviert, un-
umfürsorgt? Am
Leben?),

Lesestationen im Spätwort,

Sparflammenpunkte
am Himmel,

Kammlinien unter Beschuß,

Gefühle, frost-
gespindelt,

Kaltstart –
mit Hämoglobin.

LEAP-CENTURIES, leap-
seconds, leap-
births, novembering, leap-
deaths,

stacked in honeycomb troughs,
"bits
on chips",

the menorah poem from Berlin,

(Unasylumed, un-
archived, un-
welfare-attended? A-
live?),

reading stations in the late word,

saving flame points
in the sky,

comb lines under fire,

feelings, frost-
mandrelled,

cold start —
with haemoglobin.

WIRK NICHT VORAUS,
sende nicht aus,
steh
herein:

durchgründet vom Nichts,
ledig allen
Gebets,
feinfügig, nach
der Vor-Schrift,
unüberholbar,

nehm ich dich auf,
statt aller
Ruhe.

DO NOT WORK AHEAD,
do not send forth,
stand
into it, enter:

transfounded by nothingness,
unburdened of all
prayer,
microstructured in heeding
the pre-script,
unovertakable,

I make you at home,
instead of all
rest.

FROM
Schneepart

(1971)

BRUNNENGRÄBER im Wind:

es wird einer die Bratsche spielen, tagabwärts, im Krug,
es wird einer kopfstehn im Wort Genug,
es wird einer kreuzbeinig hängen im Tor, bei der Winde.

Dies Jahr
rauscht nicht hinüber,
es stürzt den Dezember zurück, den November,
es gräbt seine Wunden um,
es öffnet sich dir, junger
Gräber-
brunnen,
Zwölfmund.

DAS ANGEBROCHENE JAHR
mit dem modernden Kanten
Wahnbrot.

Trink
aus meinem Mund.

326

WELL-DIGGER in the wind:

someone will play the viola, downday, at the pub,
someone will stand on his head in the word Enough,
someone will hang crosslegged in the gateway, next to the
    bindweed.

This year
does not roar across,
it hurls back December, November,
it turns the soil of its wounds,
it opens to you, young
grave-
well,
twelvemouthed.

THE BROACHED YEAR
with its mouldering crusts
of delusion bread.

Drink
from my mouth.

UNLESBARKEIT dieser
Welt. Alles doppelt.

Die starken Uhren
geben der Spaltstunde recht,
heiser.

Du, in dein Tiefstes geklemmt,
entsteigst dir
für immer.

HURIGES SONST. Und die Ewigkeit
blutschwarz umbabelt.

Vermurt
von deinen lehmigen Locken
mein Glaube.

Zwei Finger, handfern,
errudern den moorigen
Schwur.

ILLEGIBILITY
of this world. All things twice over.

The strong clocks justify
the splitting hour,
hoarsely.

You, clamped
into your deepest part,
climb out of yourself
for ever.

WHORISH OTHERTIME. And eternity
babelled around the edges, bloodblack.

Mud-covered
with your loamy locks
my faith.

Two fingers, far from a hand,
row their way towards the swampy
vow.

ICH HÖRE, DIE AXT HAT GEBLÜHT,
ich höre, der Ort ist nicht nennbar,

ich höre, das Brot, das ihn ansieht,
heilt den Erhängten,
das Brot, das ihm die Frau buk,

ich höre, sie nennen das Leben
die einzige Zuflucht.

MIT DER STIMME DER FELDMAUS
quiekst du herauf,

eine scharfe
Klammer,
beißt du dich mir durchs Hemd in die Haut,

ein Tuch,
gleitest du mir auf den Mund,
mitten in meiner
dich Schatten beschwerenden
Rede.

I HEAR THAT THE AXE HAS FLOWERED,
I hear that the place can't be named,

I hear that the bread which looks at him
heals the hanged man,
the bread baked for him by his wife,

I hear that they call life
our only refuge.

WITH THE VOICE OF THE FIELDMOUSE
you squeak up to me,

a sharp
clip,
you bite your way through my shirt to the skin,

a cloth,
you slide across my mouth
midway through the words
I address to you, shadow,
to give you weight.

DIE NACHZUSTOTTERNDE WELT,
bei der ich zu Gast
gewesen sein werde, ein Name,
herabgeschwitzt von der Mauer,
an der eine Wunde hochleckt.

EINGEJÄNNERT
in der bedornten
Balme. (Betrink dich
und nenn sie
Paris.)

Frostgesiegelt die Schulter;
stille
Schuttkäuze drauf;
Buchstaben zwischen den Zehen;
Gewißheit.

WORLD TO BE STUTTERED BY HEART
in which
I shall have been a guest, a name
sweated down from the wall
a wound licks up.

JANUARIED
into the thorn-covered
rock recess. (Get drunk
and call it
Paris.)

My shoulder frost-sealed;
silent
rubble owls perched on it;
letters between my toes;
certainty.

LARGO

Gleichsinnige du, heidegängerisch Nahe:

über-
sterbens-
groß liegen
wir beieinander, die Zeit-
lose wimmelt
dir unter den atmenden Lidern,

das Amselpaar hängt
neben uns, unter
unsern gemeinsam droben mit-
ziehenden weißen

Meta-
stasen.

LARGO

You of the same mind, moor-wandering near one:

more-than-
death-
sized we lie
together, autumn
crocus, the timeless, teems
under our breathing eyelids,

the pair of blackbirds hangs
beside us, under
our whitely drifting
companions up there, our

meta-
stases.

MAPESBURY ROAD

Die dir zugewinkte
Stille von hinterm
Schritt einer Schwarzen.

Ihr zur Seite
die
magnolienstündige Halbuhr
vor einem Rot,
das auch anderswo Sinn sucht –
oder auch nirgends.

Der volle
Zeithof um
einen Steckschuß, daneben, hirnig.

Die scharfgehimmelten höfigen
Schlucke Mitluft.

Vertag dich nicht, du.

MAPESBURY ROAD

The stillness waved
at you from behind
a black woman's gait.

At her side
the
magnolia-houred halfclock
in front of a red
that elsewhere too looks for its meaning –
or nowhere perhaps.

The full
time-yard around
a lodged bullet, next to it, cerebrous.

The sharply-heavened courtyardy
gulps of co-air.

Don't adjourn yourself, you.

EIN BLATT, baumlos
für Bertolt Brecht:

Was sind das für Zeiten,
wo ein Gespräch
beinah ein Verbrechen ist,
weil es soviel Gesagtes
mit einschließt?

BERGUNG allen
Abwässerglucksens
im Briefmarken-Unken-
ruf. Cor-
respondenz.

Euphorisierte
Zeitlupenchöre behirnter
Zukunftssaurier
heizen ein Selbstherz.

Dessen
Abstoß, ich wintre
zu dir über.

A LEAF, treeless
for Bertolt Brecht:

What times are these
when a conversation
is almost a crime
because it includes
so much made explicit?

SALVAGING of all
waste water gurglings
in postage stamp frog-
calls. Cor-
respondence.

Euphorized
slow motion choruses of bebrained
saurians of the future
heat up a selfheart.

Its
push-off, I'm wintering
over to you.

From
Zeitgehöft
(1976)

WANDERSTAUDE, du fängst dir
eine der Reden,

die abgeschworene Aster
stößt hier hinzu,

wenn einer, der
die Gesänge zerschlug,
jetzt spräche zum Stab,
seine und aller
Blendung
bliebe aus.

ERST WENN ich dich
als Schatten berühre,
glaubst du mir meinen
Mund,

der klettert mit Spät-
sinnigem droben
in Zeithöfen
umher,

du stößt zur Heerschar
der Zweitverwerter unter
den Engeln,

Schweigewütiges
sternt.

WALKING PLANT, you catch
yourself one of the speeches,

the abjured aster
here joins in,

if one who
smashed the canticles
were now to speak to the staff
his and everyone's
blinding
would be revoked.

NOT UNTIL
as a shade I touch you
will you believe
my mouth,

that clambers about
with late-minded things
up there
in time-courts,

you come to the host
of the seconds-utilizers among
the angels,

and a body that rages for silence
stars.

ALLE DIE SCHLAFGESTALTEN, kristallin,
die du annahmst
im Sprachschatten,

ihnen
führ ich mein Blut zu,

die Bildzeilen, sie
soll ich bergen
in den Schlitzvenen
meiner Erkenntnis –,

meine Trauer, ich seh's,
läuft zu dir über.

KLEINE NACHT: wenn du
mich hinnimmst, hinnimmst,
hinauf,
drei Leidzoll überm
Boden:

alle die Sterbemäntel aus Sand,
alle die Helfenichtse,
alles, was da noch
lacht
mit der Zunge –

ALL THOSE SLEEP SHAPES, crystalline,
that you assumed
in the language shadow,

to those
I lead my blood,

those image lines, them
I'm to harbour
in the slit-arteries
of my cognition –,

my grief, I can see,
is deserting to you.

LITTLE NIGHT: when you
take me inside, take me
up there,
three pain-inches above the
floor:

all those shroud coats of sand,
all those can'thelps,
all that still
laughs
with the tongue –

ICH ALBERE mit meiner Nacht,
wir kapern
alles,
was sich hier losriß,

lad du mir auch deine
Finsternis auf
die halben, fahrenden
Augen,

auch sie soll es hören,
von überallher,
das unwiderlegbare Echo
jeder Verschattung.

I FOOL ABOUT with my night,
we capture
all
that tore loose here,

your darkness too
load on to
my halved, voyaging
eyes,

it too is to hear it
from every direction,
the incontrovertible echo
of every eclipse.

EIN STERN
lauscht einem Licht,
eine Stunde verstößt
eine Stunde,

herzschwer
rollt Azur
über dich hin,

dein blutiger
Speichel
beglückt
ein besessenes Staubkorn,

ein Mutterstummel
führt ein Frühgesicht
durch einen Schmerz,

sein Gott
schreitet mähend die Bilderfront ab,
auf den Graten
der obersten
Wiege.

A STAR
listens to a light,
an hour casts out
an hour,

heart-heavy,
azure rolls
along over you,

your bloody
saliva
gives joy
to a grain of dust that's possessed,

a mother stump
leads a new-born face
through a pain,

its god
mowing musters the picture front
on the ridges
of the highest
cradle.

DIE POSAUNENSTELLE
tief im glühenden
Leertext,
in Fackelhöhe,
im Zeitloch:

hör dich ein
mit dem Mund.

THE TRUMPET PART
deep in the glowing
lacuna
at lamp height
in the time hole:

listen your way in
with your mouth.

DIE POLE
sind in uns,
unübersteigbar
im Wachen,
wir schlafen hinüber, vors Tor
des Erbarmens,

ich verliere dich an dich, das
ist mein Schneetrost,

sag, daß Jerusalem *ist*,

sags, als wäre ich dieses
dein Weiß,
als wärst du
meins,

als könnten wir ohne uns wir sein,

ich blättre dich auf, für immer,

du betest, du bettest
uns frei.

THE POLES
are inside us,
insurmountable
when we're awake,
we sleep across, up to the Gate
of Mercy,

I lose you to you, that
is my snowy comfort,

say that Jerusalem *is*,

say it, as though I were this
your whiteness,
as though you
were mine,

as though without us we could be we,

I open your leaves, for ever,

you pray, you bed
us free.

Index of German Titles or First Lines

355

Index of English Titles or First Lines

READ MORE IN PENGUIN

In every corner of the world, on every subject under the sun, Penguin represents quality and variety – the very best in publishing today.

For complete information about books available from Penguin – including Puffins, Penguin Classics and Arkana – and how to order them, write to us at the appropriate address below. Please note that for copyright reasons the selection of books varies from country to country.

In the United Kingdom: Please write to *Dept. EP, Penguin Books Ltd, Bath Road, Harmondsworth, West Drayton, Middlesex UB7 ODA*

In the United States: Please write to *Consumer Sales, Penguin Putnam Inc., P.O. Box 12289 Dept. B, Newark, New Jersey 07101-5289*. VISA and MasterCard holders call 1-800-788-6262 to order Penguin titles

In Canada: Please write to *Penguin Books Canada Ltd, 10 Alcorn Avenue, Suite 300, Toronto, Ontario M4V 3B2*

In Australia: Please write to *Penguin Books Australia Ltd, P.O. Box 257, Ringwood, Victoria 3134*

In New Zealand: Please write to *Penguin Books (NZ) Ltd, Private Bag 102902, North Shore Mail Centre, Auckland 10*

In India: Please write to *Penguin Books India Pvt Ltd, 11 Community Centre, Panchsheel Park, New Delhi 110017*

In the Netherlands: Please write to *Penguin Books Netherlands bv, Postbus 3507, NL-1001 AH Amsterdam*

In Germany: Please write to *Penguin Books Deutschland GmbH, Metzlerstrasse 26, 60594 Frankfurt am Main*

In Spain: Please write to *Penguin Books S. A., Bravo Murillo 19, 1° B, 28015 Madrid*

In Italy: Please write to *Penguin Italia s.r.l., Via Benedetto Croce 2, 20094 Corsico, Milano*

In France: Please write to *Penguin France, Le Carré Wilson, 62 rue Benjamin Baillaud, 31500 Toulouse*

In Japan: Please write to *Penguin Books Japan Ltd, Kaneko Building, 2-3-25 Koraku, Bunkyo-Ku, Tokyo 112*

In South Africa: Please write to *Penguin Books South Africa (Pty) Ltd, Private Bag X14, Parkview, 2122 Johannesburg*

READ MORE IN PENGUIN

Penguin Twentieth-Century Classics offer a selection of the finest works of literature published this century. Spanning the globe from Argentina to America, from France to India, the masters of prose and poetry are represented by Penguin.

If you would like a catalogue of the Twentieth-Century Classics library, please write to:

Penguin Press Marketing, 27 Wrights Lane, London W8 5TZ

(Available while stocks last)

READ MORE IN PENGUIN

A CHOICE OF TWENTIETH-CENTURY CLASSICS

Ulysses James Joyce

Ulysses is unquestionably one of the supreme masterpieces, in any artistic form, of the twentieth century. 'It is the book to which we are all indebted and from which none of us can escape' T. S. Eliot

The First Man Albert Camus

'It is the most brilliant semi-autobiographical account of an Algerian childhood amongst the grinding poverty and stoicism of poor French-Algerian colonials' J. G. Ballard. 'A kind of magical Rosetta stone to his entire career, illuminating both his life and his work with stunning candour and passion' *The New York Times*

Flying Home Ralph Ellison

Drawing on his early experience – his father's death when he was three, hoboeing his way on a freight train to follow his dream of becoming a musician – Ellison creates stories which, according to the *Washington Post*, 'approach the simple elegance of Chekhov.' 'A shining instalment' *The New York Times Book Review*

Cider with Rosie Laurie Lee

'Laurie Lee's account of childhood and youth in the Cotswolds remains as fresh and full of joy and gratitude for youth and its sensations as when it first appeared. It sings in the memory' *Sunday Times*. 'A work of art' Harold Nicolson

Kangaroo D. H. Lawrence

Escaping from the decay and torment of post-war Europe, Richard and Harriett Somers arrive in Australia to a new and freer life. Somers, a disillusioned writer, becomes involved with an extreme political group. At its head is the enigmatic Kangaroo.

READ MORE IN PENGUIN

A CHOICE OF TWENTIETH-CENTURY CLASSICS

Belle du Seigneur   Albert Cohen

Belle du Seigneur is one of the greatest love stories in modern literature. It is also a hilarious mock-epic concerning the mental world of the cuckold. 'A *tour de force*, a comic masterpiece weighted with an understanding of human frailty ... It is, quite simply, a book that must be read' *Observer*.

The Diary of a Young Girl   Anne Frank

'Fifty years have passed since Anne Frank's diary was first published. Her story came to symbolize not only the travails of the Holocaust, but the struggle of the human spirit ... This edition is a worthy memorial' *The Times*. 'A witty, funny and tragic book ... stands on its own even without its context of horror' *Sunday Times*

Herzog   Saul Bellow

'A feast of language, situations, characters, ironies, and a controlled moral intelligence ... Bellow's rapport with his central character seems to me novel writing in the grand style of a Tolstoy – subjective, complete, heroic' *Chicago Tribune*

The Go-Between   L. P. Hartley

Discovering an old diary, Leo, now in his sixties, is drawn back to the hot summer of 1900 and his visit to Brandham Hall ... 'An intelligent, complex and beautifully-felt evocation of nascent boyhood sexuality that is also a searching exploration of the nature of memory and myth' Douglas Brooks-Davies

Orlando   Virginia Woolf

Sliding in and out of three centuries, and slipping between genders, Orlando is the sparkling incarnation of the personality of Vita Sackville-West as Virginia Woolf saw it.

READ MORE IN PENGUIN

A CHOICE OF TWENTIETH-CENTURY CLASSICS

Collected Stories Vladimir Nabokov

Here, for the first time in paperback, the stories of one of the twentieth century's greatest prose stylists are collected in a single volume. 'To read him in full flight is to experience stimulation that is at once intellectual, imaginative and aesthetic, the nearest thing to pure sensual pleasure that prose can offer' Martin Amis

Cancer Ward Aleksandr Solzhenitsyn

Like his hero Oleg Kostoglotov, Aleksandr Solzhenitsyn spent many years in labour camps for mocking Stalin and was eventually transferred to a cancer ward. 'What he has done above all things is record the truth in such a manner as to render it indestructible, stamping it into the Western consciousness' *Observer*

Nineteen Eighty-Four George Orwell

'A volley against the authoritarian in every personality, a polemic against every orthodoxy, an anarchistic blast against every un-questioning conformist ... *Nineteen Eighty-Four* is a great novel, and it will endure because its message is a permanent one' Ben Pimlott

The Complete Saki Saki

Macabre, acid and very funny, Saki's work drives a knife into the upper crust of English Edwardian life. Here are the effete and dashing heroes, Reginald, Clovis and Comus Bassington, tea on the lawn, the smell of gunshot and the tinkle of the caviar fork, and here is the half-seen, half-felt menace of disturbing undercurrents ...

The Castle Franz Kafka

'In *The Castle* we encounter a proliferation of obstacles, endless conversations, perpetual possibilities which hook on to each other as if intent to go on until the end of time' Idris Parry. 'Kafka may be the most important writer of the twentieth century' J. G. Ballard

READ MORE IN PENGUIN

A SELECTION OF POETRY

Octavio Paz   Selected Poems

'His poetry allows us to glimpse a different and future place ... liberating and affirming' *Guardian*

Allen Ginsberg   Collected Poems 1947–1985

'Ginsberg is responsible for loosening the breath of American poetry at mid-century' *New Yorker*

Jules Laforgue   Selected Poems

During a tragically short life, Jules Laforgue created a poetic persona so powerful it decisively influenced the work of T. S. Eliot and Ezra Pound, marking him out as one of the founding fathers of modernism.

Roger McGough   Sporting Relations

'McGough's knack, as the Peoples' Poet Laureate, is to be relevant and contemporary; to achieve popularity without patronising' Clare Henry, *Glasgow Herald*

Fernando Pessoa   Selected Poems

'I have sought for his shade in those Edwardian cafés in Lisbon which he haunted, for he was Lisbon's Cavafy or Verlaine' *Sunday Times*

John Updike   Collected Poems 1953–1993

'Updike's eye comes up very close ... yet eschews the gruesome, keeps life vivid and slippery and erotic' *Observer*

Craig Charles   No Other Blue

Actor and comedian Craig Charles reveals yet another talent with his first collection of poetry.

Penguin Modern Poets

This highly influential series celebrates the best and most innovative of today's poetic voices.